W9-BDZ-853

The World's Endangered Wildlife

The World's Endangered Wildlife

George Laycock

Illustrated with photographs

A THISTLE BOOK
Published by

GROSSET & DUNLAP, INC.
A National General Company
New York

Library of Congress Catalog Card No. 72-92928
ISBN: 0-448-26237-1

Printed in the United States of America

762597

4.95

Bound

12-31-73

ACKNOWLEDGMENTS

The author wishes to extend his appreciation to the numerous organizations and individuals who generously gave him assistance during preparation of this book. Special thanks are due the following persons for their kindness in supplying information or reviewing all or portions of the completed manuscript: Dr. F. Wayne King, Curator of Herpetology, New York Zoological Park; Edward Maruska, Director Cincinnati Zoo; Stephen R. Seater, Staff Biologist, World Wildlife Fund; Dr. Randall L. Eaton, School of Forest Resources, University of Georgia; and Earl Basinger, Office of Endangered Species, U.S. Bureau of Sport Fisheries and Wildlife.

Cover photograph by Ron Garrison
Courtesy San Diego Zoo
Siberian Tigers
(*Panthera tigris*)

About the Author

GEORGE LAYCOCK, a native of Ohio, has a degree in wildlife management from the Ohio State University. He served in the Army for three and a half years, including twenty months in Europe, where he was commissioned during World War II.

After graduation from Ohio State he joined the staff of *Farm Quarterly* as associate editor, a post he held for four and a half years. He resigned in 1951 to devote his full time to writing.

Since that time Mr. Laycock has written hundreds of articles for such magazines as *Better Homes and Gardens, Field and Stream, Outdoor Life, Sports Afield, Boys' Life, Audubon, National Wildlife,* and several others. He serves as a field editor of *Audubon.* Many of his articles have been illustrated with his own photographs. He has also written numerous books on natural history and the environment. In the course of his research, Mr. Laycock has traveled widely over North and South America, and Africa. Mr. and Mrs. Laycock, who have three grown children, live in Cincinnati, Ohio.

CONTENTS

CHAPTER 1

The Disappearing Wildlife

ONE SEPTEMBER DAY in 1914, a rare bird sat silently on her perch. She was old and sick and weak. That day the bird slipped from the roost and lay dead on the floor of the cage in the zoo at Cincinnati, Ohio.

Usually a bird can die and no one pays much attention to it. But this one was gathered up tenderly and sent off to Washington, D.C. There, in the Smithsonian Institution, she was expertly mounted. She has been seen by thousands of people. Her name was "Martha," and the thing that was unusual about Martha was that she was the very last passenger pigeon known to be living anywhere in the world.

It was hard to believe that the world would never see another living passenger pigeon. Less than a hundred years earlier, the skies had been darkened by passenger pigeons. They moved across the land in flocks that some-

1

The rare brow-antlered deer of India.

times flew endlessly over the fields and forests for days at a time. There were millions of them, so many that they were killed and taken by the wagonload to market.

It is too late now to help the passenger pigeon. Neither can we help other species that have vanished. The world's wildlife is becoming extinct faster than ever before within man's memory. In the past fifty years, an average of one vertebrate species has become extinct each year. This means that the rate of extinction has doubled within the last two centuries.

Man has changed the world around him. As the human population increased, new lands were cleared, lakes and streams were polluted, and wildlife was often killed carelessly without thinking about leaving some to keep the species alive. More and more, we have crowded the earth. We have continued to change it steadily. The earth no longer looks as it once did. The wild creatures have seen the world changed and their living space destroyed.

In recent times, more and more people have begun working to save the wildlife. Within the United States Government, workers in the U.S. Bureau of Sport Fisheries and Wildlife published a book listing the endangered species. Meanwhile, endangered species around the world are listed in other books. These are called the Red Data Books, and they are a roster of wildlife in trouble everywhere. The organization that keeps this list is the International Union for the Conservation of Nature, the IUCN.

Others are also working to help the endangered species. Nations and states have refuges and sanctuaries for wildlife. So do some industries that own land, and some private landowners as well. Everywhere people are learning more about the troubles faced by wildlife in the modern world.

The Indian one-horned rhinoceros has suffered from poaching.

Peregrine falcons have vanished from most of their range
because chemicals in the environment cause them to produce eggs that cannot hatch or young that fail to survive.

The news is sad. According to the IUCN, in April 1971, the world had 922 species of fish, amphibians, reptiles, birds and mammals threatened with extinction. And the list is still growing.

But there are others not even on this list. There are invertebrates, such as insects and mollusks, being wiped out by chemicals, dam-building and other changes we make in the environment. Meanwhile, there also are many plants threatened with extinction.

Why should people worry about wildlife becoming extinct? Think first about why the animals can no longer live. Their world has changed. Men who worked in coal mines deep under the surface of the earth once carried a canary in a cage with them into the mines when they went to work. The miners worried about poisonous gases that might kill them. Such gases, they learned, would kill canaries first. If the canary died, the miners knew they must hurry out into the fresh air. The canary was their early warning system.

Biologists explain that when wildlife dies an unnatural death, men should take warning. A world that is no longer fit for the wild creatures to live in might also become unfit for people. The wildlife around us is our canary in the mine shaft.

But there are other reasons for saving the wildlife from extinction. Every living organism is part of an ecosystem where different species survive together. When one of these species vanishes, the world is also changed for other plants and animals around it. Each time another species disappears the world is a little bit poorer. The outdoors loses some more of its interesting forms of life.

Let us meet some of the animals which are in danger and think about the world without them if we should fail to rescue them in time.

CHAPTER 2

Orangutan

LATE IN THE afternoon, when shadows probe like long fingers through the jungle, an orangutan swings among the treetops. He comes upon some fruit of the durian, pulls the husks away, and eats. His hunger is gone now, daylight is failing, and the great red ape looks around for a place to spend the night.

Soon he begins gathering branches and arranging them into a platform on the fork of a tree. The work goes on and finally the bed is lined with a layer of leaves. Here the orang snuggles lazily into the leafy bed, curls up and falls asleep. Nearby, a little group of females and young have also nested for the night in their jungle treehouses.

Full-grown, the wild orangutan may weigh as much as 300 pounds. If he were to stand up straight, which he seldom does, he might measure four feet tall and look almost as broad as he is tall. His massive shoulders and

powerful arms carry great reserves of strength. His arms are so long that from fingertip to fingertip he has a seven- to eight-foot reach.

When walking, the orangutan places his knuckles on the ground and swings the weight of his massive body forward between his arms as if they were crutches.

But he is seldom in a hurry. By nature he takes life easy. In the jungle he has no special place to go and no scheduled time to get there. He relaxes a lot and leads what would seem to be an ideal life, climbing trees, building treehouses, and eating fresh fruit, hand-picked in the high places.

Orangutans are not particularly early risers. When the other wild creatures around them awaken at dawn, the big apes slumber on, perhaps until eight o'clock or so, and sometimes stay in bed until almost noon. Then, after lunch, they may return to their nest for another nap. They may spend more than half the daylight hours resting and sleeping.

In color, the long, shaggy orangutan is a dark reddish brown. Old males may develop large, flabby bags of skin that hang beneath their chins and their faces.

When they are four years old, the females are sexually mature, and they may remain capable of reproducing for the following twenty or twenty-five years. This would seem to give them a potential for producing numerous young, but each female has only one young every four years. In addition, there is such a high rate of infant

◀Orangutan, the lazy ape, lives only on the islands of Sumatra and Borneo, or in captivity like this one.
COURTESY CINCINNATI ZOO

mortality that the female may add only two or three young to the population.

During the infant's first months the mother keeps it cuddled close to her. But by the time the youngster is a year and a half old, it is learning to gather branches and leaves to build its own nest each evening. In their tree-top world there should be peace and safety for the orangutan. But its world today is filled with threats.

All the other great apes of the world live in Africa. But the orangutan lives only on the islands of Sumatra and Borneo. And on these islands its forest home is shrinking before the chopping and whining of axes and saws. The orangutan lives in the lowlands, mostly below elevations of 2,500 feet, and in old forests that have stood for ages. As these primary forests are timbered, the orangutans must go to higher country, and there the fruit on which they live is seldom as abundant as it was in the lowlands.

This habitat destruction has cut heavily into their numbers. But it is only one of the reasons why the orangutan is in danger. Until very recently there has been a heavy demand for them in zoos around the world, especially in Europe and America. Because there is no easy way to capture a full-grown, wild orangutan, the hunter searches out a female carrying an infant. Then he shoots the mother so he can safely capture her baby.

Quite often the young orangutan, like the mother, is killed by mistake, or by the body of the mother falling on it as she crashes out of the treetops. Even if the baby orangutan is still alive and well, it may later catch a human disease and die. So, for each one brought into captivity, perhaps three others have died.

The infant orangs are carried out of the dense, green

jungles to cities such as Singapore, then smuggled aboard ships bound for distant ports and waiting buyers.

Because the orangutan is so rare and its survival critically endangered, directors of large and responsible zoos in the United States will no longer buy one anywhere without the approval of the American Association of Zoological Parks and Aquariums.

But timbering, poaching and smuggling still cut into their dwindling numbers.

To save the orangutan, some zoologists believe there should be large refuges for them in their native islands. In such sanctuaries, they would be protected from poaching and from the destruction of their mature forests.

Others believe zoos offer the best chance and hope that someday orangs born in captivity may be released to repopulate the jungles where they have become so rare.

Everglade kite at the nest. This bird is a hawk, with a
strong liking for the apple snail.

COURTESY P. W. SYKES, JR.
U.S. BUREAU OF SPORT FISHERIES AND WILDLIFE

CHAPTER 3

The Everglade Kite

ONE WINTER DAY a visitor stopped on the west side of a large lake in Florida. He hoped to see a rare bird that few people ever see. Waiting to meet him was a warden for the National Audubon Society. The warden's job was to guard the rare birds.

A few minutes later, they were in the warden's airboat skimming over the shallow water of Lake Okeechobee. There was a strong wind in their faces, and rows of spray made long, white trails on either side of the speeding boat. The airboat is just right for this job. It will run on water so shallow that a regular outboard motor would drag the bottom. It is driven by an airplane motor and propeller. Its broad, flat bottom glides across the mud flats and the grassy marshes.

After several miles, the airboat scooted through a narrow, grassy channel. It came out into a little place where the water stood calm and still, surrounded by walls of grass and sedges. The airboat stopped, and the warden turned the engine off. Then he pointed to a dark bird flying low over the shallow lake far off to the north. Now the visitor had seen his first Everglade kite, one of the rarest birds in the world.

This bird is a hawk, sometimes called the "snail kite," because the only food it will eat is the apple snail which lives in the shallow water in some parts of Florida. The northern visitor watched the snail kite until it came close enough to be studied through the binoculars.

It flew over the water about twenty feet above the surface of the lake. "It's hunting for snails," said the Audubon warden. "Watch it when it sees one." The bird was looking downward into the water as it flew. "The snails feed on the soft, muddy bottom of the lake," the warden explained. "Then they climb up the stems of grass and rest a few inches beneath the surface. Now, watch," he said.

The kite had turned and come back for a better look at something it had spotted in the water. "It can tell if the snail is dead in its shell," the warden said. "If it is, the kite doesn't go after it, but flies off instead and looks for others."

But the kite quickly dropped down close to the water. It hovered for a few seconds as the visitor watched it closely through his binoculars. Then it reached one foot into the water and grasped something. When it flew slowly away over the lake, it carried the snail in one foot. The bird had captured the snail without even wetting its feathers. It shifted the snail to its bill, then settled on a perch in the top of a dead bush about ten feet above the water.

Opening a snail's shell is not an easy task. A man

would need the help of a knife to do it. But the kite
has a long, hooked bill, and it began at once to work
on the snail. Soon, by using its feet and bill, it had
picked the flesh of the snail from its shell and eaten it.
Next, it wiped first one side of its bill, then the other,
on the perch and removed the sticky fluids left there by
the snail.

As the bird rested in the full sunlight, the visitor had
a fine opportunity to make notes on the appearance of
the rare kite. When it flies slowly over the wetlands on
its broad wings, the Everglade kite resembles the common marsh hawk. The male kite, somewhat smaller than
its mate, is about 16 or 18 inches long and has a wing-
spread of about 44 inches. It is not a bird of beautiful
colors. Instead, it has a charcoal-colored back, and its
head and the tips of its wings are black. The eyes are
bright red and so are the legs. The female, however, has
yellowish legs and colors that are even duller than those
of her mate. She is brownish on her upper parts and
streaked with white and brown on her head and under-
parts.

In winter, before the birds begin their nesting for the
year, the male bird may be seen flying around its territory carrying a stick in its mouth. This is a courtship
display. At other times, especially when the winds are
good for soaring, he may climb far into the sky. Then
he half-folds his wings and hurtles down from the sky
at his top speed as if to impress the female.

For a nest the kites construct a platform of dry wil-
low and other sticks, then line it with grasses, leaves,
and vines. When completed it may be nearly a foot thick
and perhaps 16 inches across, perched in the brush three
to seven feet above the water. There the female lays two
or three eggs.

But this is a hazardous time for the kites, a season

when the nest and the eggs or the young may perish for any of several reasons. There was a time, years ago, when these birds lived around the shallow lakes and marshes over much of Florida. Then men began draining the wetlands. This destroyed the habitat where the kites hunted for the snails they needed.

Meanwhile, many of the kites were shot. Usually those who shoot them do not have a real reason to do so, except that the hawks are there and they fly slowly enough to be an easy target.

Sometimes, instead of there being not enough water for the kites, there is too much. Heavy rains during the nesting season may chill the young or the eggs and destroy them. Predators also sometimes take their toll of both the young and the eggs.

Of all these problems, however, none has made as much trouble for the kites as drainage. Today the kites are found in only a few places. Some live on Lake Okeechobee. Others are found on the Loxahatchee National Wildlife Refuge. They are also seen in Everglades National Park.

What can be done to save the Everglade kites from extinction? When you travel around the parts of Florida where these birds live, you may see posters with pictures of the kites and warnings against shooting them. The State of Florida, the National Audubon Society, and the U.S. Bureau of Sport Fisheries and Wildlife have all worked to tell people about the danger this bird faces and to stop the shooting. The Audubon warden has patrolled the kite nesting areas for many years to protect the rare birds.

When water is lowered or raised in Florida's water basins, the engineers must ask themselves how the change will affect the Everglade kites. In one recent year the kites had moved into the big Loxahatchee National Wildlife Refuge until forty-six birds were using the area. This was more kites on Loxahatchee than any time since the refuge was begun many years earlier. Then suddenly, and without warning, the water level dropped more than three feet. This came as a surprise to the refuge manager as well as to the kites. The engineers who had drained the area were concerned more with irrigation water than with wildlife. With the water gone, the marshes dried up. When this happens, the apple snails go underground and become inactive until water returns. With the snails gone and their hunting grounds dry, the kites left. They did not come back all summer.

The U.S. Bureau of Sport Fisheries and Wildlife has sent a wildlife biologist to Florida to study the kites and find ways to help them avoid extinction. Among his earliest jobs was counting these birds to see how many there were still living in Florida. By late in 1970, he reported that there were about 120, a figure so low that the Everglade kite is now one of the world's rarest birds.

No matter what causes the death of even one of these hawks with the strange eating habits, the loss is serious. Within a few years both the kites and the snails they eat could be gone.

The whooping crane, however, was once down to much lower numbers than the kites. And the whooping cranes are still not extinct. Everyone everywhere became concerned about them. The same kind of concern must be felt for the Everglade kite, and others. Unless we really want to rescue an endangered species from extinction and leave room for it to live with us on earth, its chances for surviving are slim.

Bengal tiger. These magnificent creatures are in danger of extinction. COURTESY GEORGE LAYCOCK

CHAPTER 4

Tigers

THE TIGER IS said to be the largest of all the cats, a giant creature draped in yellowish fur with black sidebars breaking up the solid colors and forming a pattern that melts into the jungle shadows.

A young buffalo, feeding along the edge of the lowland marsh, is unaware that the hunting tiger is nearby. The huge cat, perhaps more than nine feet long and weighing 500 pounds, moves as silently as its little cousin, the house cat. Each padded foot lifts, then is silently placed against the ground again. The long, muscular body of the giant cat inches closer.

Still the buffalo does not sense its mortal danger. The heavy, black creature stops once, lifts its head quickly. All is peace and silence. Reassured, it goes back to feeding. Now, like a trap set to spring, the tiger lowers its long, furry body and creeps forward for its final leap.

Tigers get into trouble when their natural prey is killed
by man and they then turn to man's domestic stock.

Even for the biggest cats in the world, life is not simple. At the moment of the kill the tiger himself sometimes becomes the victim. Wild boars have been known to rip open the soft bodies of attacking tigers, with furious, lightning sweeps of their sharp and powerful tusks. Whatever the prey, the tiger must be a skillful and cautious hunter or go without food.

The cat comes from the grass in one smooth, bounding motion. The buffalo, having believed itself all alone, now finds its ancient, mortal enemy leaping upon it. The buffalo veers sideways and scrambles in wild panic to escape, but it is too late. The cat sends teeth and claws into the neck as the force of its leap brings the buffalo to earth.

However, those creatures at the top of the food pyramid are often among the most seriously endangered in the modern world. Because they are big predators by nature, men often see them as enemies and kill them.

In addition, the large predators are naturally fewer in number than the little creatures which serve as their prey. Eagles are fewer than rabbits, foxes fewer than mice, tigers fewer than deer or water buffalo. And it has always been this way.

Besides, the larger the animal, the smaller the number of young it is likely to have, and the longer time it needs to bring them to maturity. The tigers take longer to replace their losses than do rabbits, mice or squirrels.

Although millions of people have seen the sleek and beautiful tigers in zoos, most of us have never seen them living in their natural habitat. The chances of seeing a tiger in the wild are becoming rarer every day. Men who have studied the big cats fear that almost everywhere they are still found, they are headed for extinction.

There are seven races of tigers in the wild, all of them

in Asia. The one least endangered is the Bengal tiger, the one most often seen in the zoo. All the others are at critically low levels. And the Bengal tiger, too, is said by the World Wildlife Fund to be in great danger.

What causes the tiger's troubles? Perhaps most important is the destruction of its habitat. Forests where the tigers live are being cut down. In addition, river bottoms and hillsides are being cleared for farming and grazing, and this reduces the living space for the wild deer on which tigers feed. Tigers may begin killing livestock instead, and then the farmer uses guns and poisons, trying to kill the tiger. Today the native people also have more guns available than they once had and more four-wheel-drive vehicles to take them where they can kill both the big cats and the animals on which they prey.

Tigers never were plentiful in the same sense that smaller animals are numerous. These big cats are solitary creatures, roaming over large, individual territories. The male may need a territory ten to twelve miles wide.

The females hunt constantly to kill enough food for their growing young. Today, as human populations spread, the tigers live closer than ever to people.

The pressure on the tigers continues. What hope then is there for them? Perhaps not much at all. Some can go on living in zoos. Out in the wild, however, their guarantee for the future is in natural parks and refuges. There both the cats and their prey are safe from poaching and from the pressures that continue to push them closer and closer to extinction.

◀ The Bengal tiger has suffered from loss of habitat and overshooting.
COURTESY ERWIN A. BAUER

The rare giant panda wears a heavy coat that protects it during the cold Chinese winters.

CHAPTER 5

Giant Panda

DEEP IN THE shadowy bamboo jungles of China, near the border of Tibet where few men ever go, the female panda led her young one along a narrow trail. She stopped to eat some of the bamboo stems and leaves on which pandas live.

While she sat in the forest chewing the tough food with her powerful teeth, her roly-poly little one bounced around her, nudging her broad sides. Suddenly, before her there stood a creature she had never seen before. The noise of a shot resounded through the forest, and the mother panda lay dead on the trail.

Confused, the young one stood beside the body of its mother and the hunter rushed up and captured it. During the following days the young panda was carried for long distances. Eventually, he was put into a big cage, and he became one of the few giant pandas in a zoo anywhere in the world. He soon became the most popular animal in the zoo, and people came many miles to see this lovable-looking "Teddy bear."

People who have never seen a giant panda before are sometimes surprised by its size. When full grown, it may weigh three hundred pounds and be six feet long if you include its ridiculously short tail.

Nobody knows how many pandas are left in the bamboo forests of China, but they are believed to be rare and are therefore listed among the world's endangered animals. Until 1869, people of the western world did not even realize there was such a creature. That year, an amazed French naturalist, Père Armand David, saw the skin of a panda in China and realized that it was new to science. Other skins were then sent back to Paris. Later a few pandas were shot by curious hunters and studied by scientists.

But until 1937, no giant panda had ever been brought out of China alive. Then the Brookfield Zoo in Chicago obtained one. It was named Su-Lin, and Su-Lin became famous. In later years, a few others were sent out of China to zoos. Today most of those in captivity, perhaps twenty, live in zoos inside China, their native land, where they are much loved by the people who come to see them.

But perhaps none became more famous than Ling-Ling and Hsing-Hsing, which were given to President Richard M. Nixon by Chinese Premier Chou En-lai in 1972. These two young giant pandas were flown to America to live in the Washington National Zoo.

Deep mysteries still surround the panda. Scientists would like to know more about how they live in the bamboo forests in their native mountains.

Pandas are now believed to be members of the bear

family. Unlike other bears, a panda does not use its claws for protection, but fights instead with those powerful, crunching teeth. Neither does it hibernate, in spite of the cold winters in its native range.

Single births seem to be the rule, and the female panda possibly has only one cub every second year.

One honor that has come to the way of the giant panda has been bestowed by the World Wildlife Fund. This conservation organization works to save all rare animals around the world. For its symbol the World Wildlife Fund selected the giant panda and printed the panda's picture on all of its letterheads and circulars, to remind everyone who sees it of all the rare animals around the world.

The vicuna has been hunted for
centuries for its valuable hair.

CHAPTER 6

Vicuna

THE LITTLE HERD of graceful animals moved slowly through the open mountain meadow. Their leader was an alert old male, standing with his head held high and erect. He was almost three feet tall and might have weighed 100 pounds, with slender legs and a body shaped somewhat like that of a deer.

For a coat he wore the finest wool in the world, thick and luxurious. In ancient times, no one but the Indian rulers was allowed to wear cloth woven from it. Today suits made of the wool of the vicuna of South America may cost as much as $1,000.

The vicuna is a relative of the llama and is also related to the camel. Its home is in the high country mostly in Peru. Once it also lived in large numbers in Argentina, Bolivia and Chile, but now it is found almost exclusively in Peru.

The small herd in the meadow was disturbed. From a distance came the faint purring sound of an engine. The leader issued a sharp, whistling alarm, and every one of the animals began running across the grassy meadow.

They ran leisurely at first. But soon they were gaining speed. The noise of the four-wheel-drive vehicle grew louder as the hunters closed the distance separating them from the speeding vicuna.

Vicuna may reach speeds of 30 miles an hour. But the hunters in their cars could travel faster. The old male was racing along behind his herd, frantically urging them forward, nipping first one, then the other on the rump to make them run faster.

The car slid to a halt. One of the men leaped from it and brought the high-powered rifle to his shoulder. Taking careful aim, he caught the body of the male in his sights and squeezed the trigger. It was important that he kill the leader first.

When the male fell, the herd was without leadership. The other animals quickly lost confidence. They began milling around, confused and frightened, and within the next several minutes every one of them was dead.

The ancient Incas who inhabited South America and who also valued the wool of the vicuna so highly, did not kill the animal to obtain its coat. Instead, men, women and children herded the wild vicuna together, sheared off their wool, and then turned them free to grow new coats.

There has never been great success raising them on ranches like sheep.

By the time he is a year old, the young male vicuna is chased away from the herd. He is driven off by the old male leader. The young one may join other males and live in a bachelor's club.

Then, when strong enough, he wanders over the mountainside seeking a territory not occupied by others of his kind. Next, he begins gathering his own herd of females. After that, he will neither permit the females to leave his territory nor allow others to come into it.

The ancient roundup of the wild vicuna and the careful harvest of its wool is a custom unknown today. The ancient tribesman has been replaced by the modern poacher. He comes illegally to the vicuna herds with visions of profits in his head and a gun in his hand. One after the other, the herds have been obliterated from the high mountainsides at the top of the Andes.

How many vicuna remain to wander across these windswept slopes? In 1957, a wildlife biologist, Carl B. Koford, traveled to South America to camp in the Andes and study the vicuna. He learned that perhaps 400,000 remained. But the poachers have been active since then, and today there are perhaps no more than 15,000 of them. Unless something is done, and done quickly, to save them, say the wildlife biologists, the vicuna is certainly headed for extinction.

There is now a refuge for these animals, a safety zone, perched more than two miles above sea level, high in the Andes Mountains 300 miles southeast of the city of Lima. Here the government of Peru, seeking ways to save its famous vicuna, learned that these animals can prosper if given protection from the poachers' guns. Within the refuge, in only four years, the numbers climbed from 1,753 to 4,664. This refuge, known as Pampa Galeras, National Vicuna Reserve, is perhaps the best place in the world to see the vicuna running free today.

Outside Peru also, people are searching for ways to rescue the vicuna. The World Wildlife Fund, which struggles to rescue endangered wildlife everywhere in the world, has raised money to help the vicuna. It has dispatched biologists to South America to study the vicuna's life habits and see what can be done for the animals.

Meanwhile, conservationists work to eliminate the market for vicuna wool. Everyone who buys the wool, or wears clothing made of it, helps bring on their extinction. Without people to buy the wool, and willing to pay the high prices it commands, the poachers would have no reason to take their guns up the mountainsides to kill vicuna. And today, nobody needs the coat of the vicuna as badly as the vicuna does.

CHAPTER 7

The Bontebok

WHEN THE FIRST settlers from Europe arrived on the continent of Africa they found a wonderland of wild creatures. Among the most beautiful of all were the many kinds of antelope. They were creatures with sleek, graceful bodies, long legs, and horns of many shapes and sizes.

One that seemed more abundant than the others on the plains of South Africa was an alert creature about 44 inches high at the shoulder, wearing a coat of rich purplish red. It had pure white, knee-length "stockings." There was also white on its rump and a long splash of white down the front of its slender face. It was called the "bontebok."

This antelope furnished excellent meat and was easily hunted, and this meant trouble for the bontebok. For ages it had survived in that region of South Africa, along with its natural predators. But the coming of men with firearms and tools for farming brought a new and powerful enemy.

The bontebok began to disappear quickly. By the early 1800s people believed that this once abundant animal was about to vanish from the earth forever.

Farming and hunting continued. The rich lands where the bontebok had once thrived were no longer safe for it. Now they lived only in small herds and on the poorer lands where there was less for them to eat. The government said those who continued to kill the bontebok must pay heavy fines. But this didn't stop the hunting, and the bontebok edged still closer to that final day when only one would remain, then none at all.

Then there began one of the strangest stories in the history of Africa's amazing wildlife. A man named Alexander Van der Byl owned much land and, about 1835, he was busy building fences around some of his property. He had thought often about the bontebok, and wondered how people might save them from extinction. Most of those still living ranged over the plains not far from his farm.

Thinking about this, and looking at his new rows of fence, Mr. Van der Byl had an idea. Perhaps his plan would not work at all. No one else had ever tried it. Mr. Van der Byl reasoned that if the bontebok were living on his own lands he could protect them. Then perhaps their numbers would increase.

With this idea in mind he set off with some of his employees, and perhaps a few friends, to locate the last of the bontebok. Then they began driving the wild antelope steadily closer to the newly fenced range. According to old accounts of the event, this remarkable round-up brought about 300 of the nervous animals into Mr. Van der Byl's newly fenced range.

The bontebok is among the most beautiful of the many
kinds of antelope.   COURTESY KARL H. MASLOWSKI

The bontebok has been heavily killed for food.

Then a neighbor, seeing what Mr. Van der Byl had done, agreed that this was a good idea. He searched out some more of the last wild bontebok and brought them onto his ranch.

In the following years, those few small herds of bontebok living outside the fences continued to disappear. Almost certainly, the species would have died out completely in those years if it had not been for those living securely on the ranches. No longer were there many truly wild bontebok. What had happened to the bontebok of South Africa was about the same as what would happen in the years ahead to the bison of North America. Both would be saved, at least for the present. But they would live in herds where they would be neither wild and free, nor completely domesticated.

In 1930, when there was scarcely a wild bontebok anywhere, the government set up a small national park for the very last of them. It is known now as Bontebok National Park. That first year there were only twenty-two animals living on it. By 1953, this number was up to 120 and there were enough so that some could be safely transferred to a new park. They continued to increase.

Meanwhile, more ranchers started their own small herds of bontebok. By 1970, there were 900 of them again. This is not many bontebok when compared with the thousands that once roamed their home range.

Some people now consider that the bontebok has been saved from extinction. On the ranches and in the parks where it lives, it is safer than it has been for 150 years. But the World Wildlife Fund, which keeps close watch on endangered creatures everywhere, still speaks of the bontebok as "severely threatened."

Eggs taken from Atlantic salmon are placed in a tray in the cold water at Craig Brook Hatchery, for controlled hatching and rearing and subsequent release in Maine rivers.   COURTESY LUTHER C. GOLDMAN
U.S. BUREAU OF SPORT FISHERIES AND WILDLIFE

CHAPTER 8

Atlantic Salmon

FOR SEVERAL DAYS the young salmon had moved from pool to pool down the stream toward the ocean. Finally he came to the estuary at the edge of the sea, where the salt water and fresh mixed together. For the salmon, this was a new world. Drawn by some force he did not understand, he swam away from the river into the darkness of the rolling ocean.

He was an Atlantic salmon and what scientists call an "anadromous" fish. He had hatched in fresh water far upstream in the same stream where his parents had hatched. Then, as they had done, he would go out into the ocean with the other salmon. In a distant part of the ocean he would feed and grow until the time came to return to the stream to spawn. This was the ancient pattern of his life and a schedule only death could stop.

No one entirely understands how the Atlantic salmon

are guided through the vast, unmarked ocean. Scientists believe, however, that the fish can tell their own streams from the others by the odors of the water. In nature, no water is pure for long. It absorbs the substances through which it flows. To the salmon each stream has its own odors, and their original stream is known and remembered even after the wandering salmon have been three years at sea, when they return for their first spawning season.

For the restless salmon, life is filled with uncertainty, risk and hazards. Most of the fish around them live by eating other fish. But enough of the salmon survive the hazards of the oceans to return each year to their own streams and start another life cycle.

After three years at sea the salmon was an adult, weighing nearly ten pounds. He began moving out again on a long journey back toward the mouth of the stream in which he had hatched. For several days he stayed around the estuary. Then, with many other salmon, he began the long swim up the shallow stream toward the place from which he had come.

During the years of feeding and growing far out in the North Atlantic, the salmon becomes a strikingly beautiful fish. His back is bluish black, his sides and belly a sparkling silver color. But as he migrates over the long ocean trail back toward his own stream, his colors change. The flashing silver of his sides darkens. Within the bodies of all the adult salmon returning for the spawning, there are remarkable changes occurring. The females develop 700 or 800 eggs for each pound of their body weight. The males feel the urgency of the spawning season. All of them rush into the stream, splashing and crowding through its pools and over its riffles.

A hundred or two hundred years ago there were so many salmon in the ocean and the streams that there

This magnificent sport fish has been trapped for tagging and release for migration studies.

A fine male specimen of the Atlantic salmon.
COURTESY LUTHER C. GOLDMAN
U.S. BUREAU OF SPORT FISHERIES AND WILDLIFE

seemed to be no danger of destroying them all. Fisher-men pursued these giant prizes in the famous fishing streams on both sides of the Atlantic. One record At-lantic salmon weighed 79½ pounds.

But the salmons' way of life was a threat to their ex-istence. Officials of the countries with spawning streams could pass laws on how the fish would be caught and how many could be taken. But far off in the North At-lantic Ocean, the salmon belonged to no nation. Modern, hard-working commercial fishing boats might even take the very last of the salmon and no one would be able to stop them.

As the human population grows throughout the world, so does its need for food. People look everywhere for new sources of protein. During the 1960s a few nations began fishing the open seas for the salmon. On the island of Greenland people had long known about the beautiful and delicious salmon cruising the northern waters along its coast. As the salmon worked their way through Baffin Bay, the fishermen would set out their stake nets.

This had been going on for many years without caus-ing much damage to the salmon stocks. The fishermen took only enough for their own people, and what they took could be replaced in the next spawning season.

Then Greenland began exporting some of its catch. In 1957, two tons of the fine big salmon were sent to Denmark, to which Greenland belongs. Officials there thought of all the salmon living out in the international waters during so much of the year. Denmark has almost no salmon-spawning streams of its own. But soon new fishing boats were moving out of Denmark and Green-land and zeroing in on the Atlantic-salmon feeding grounds. During 1964, Greenland sent 1400 tons of sal-mon to market and used another 500 tons among its own people. Meanwhile, other countries started fishing for the salmon. They used nets, and they stretched long lines with hundreds of hooks on them. The numbers of salmon being removed from the Atlantic almost doubled.

In addition, enemies of the salmon, including disease, sediment and other kinds of water pollution, ruined some of their spawning waters, and some new dams have stopped them from migrating back up their streams.

No matter what the other countries said, the Danes and Greenlanders went right on sending out their fishing boats as if determined to catch and haul in the very last of the Atlantic salmon. Finally, early in 1972, the Danish government agreed to stop its high seas fishing for the salmon after four more years.

Will this save the Atlantic salmon? Some scientists have serious doubts. Perhaps the salmon can never recover. If the fishing lasts too long, the famed Atlantic salmon will become one more of the world's species to vanish.

CHAPTER 9

How the Oryx Came to Arizona

LATE IN THE day, the tracks seemed fresher. At last the hunter came to the top of a ridge. He dismounted from his camel and crawled forward to study the barren country below. There were the oryx, but still he must move in closer.

He slipped back to where his camel stood. Then, trying to walk so that he would be hidden by the camel, he came steadily closer. He could pick out the old female leader of the little herd, and the excitement grew within him. Suddenly she lifted her head. The others were alerted too. They began running off across the desert into the open spaces where they would be alone again. Sadly, the wandering hunter turned away. Many times he had hunted the oryx with his old rifle, but never yet had he come close enough to shoot one of the graceful, speeding creatures.

But new hunting methods were coming, and with them would come the threat of death for all the oryx.

Of the species of oryx in the world today, one lives in the north African deserts, another in south and east Africa. The rarest of them all, however, is the Arabian oryx. The Arabian oryx once ranged widely over the deserts of southwest Asia. Only in the southern part of their Asian range do they still survive. Perhaps there are fewer than 200 of them still running wild.

Sleek and beautiful, this wild, spirited antelope is almost white. It wears rich chocolate brown on its legs and black markings on its face. The horns, beautiful and powerful, stick nearly straight out of the top of its head. In combat, the oryx lowers its head and brings the long, stout horns nearly parallel to the ground. Then it attacks. In Africa, the oryx has been known to kill lions.

The adult oryx may weigh from 350 to 450 pounds. Why do hunters seek the oryx? The flesh is food. Besides, tribesmen have used the points of the horns as spear tips and the tough, thick hide to cover their shields.

The Arabian oryx eats herbs, grasses, and sometimes fruit or roots. Its foods are often thinly scattered, and for this reason the oryx is a wanderer. The land where it lives is dry, but it can survive for long periods on no more moisture than it obtains from its food.

As long as hunters could only stalk the oryx on foot, or with camels, these sleek, fast-running creatures were a match for any man. They could usually escape.

Then came better guns. And camels were replaced by powerful vehicles that could travel across the deserts faster than the oryx could run. Royal hunting parties, sometimes several hundred cars strong, went searching for the oryx. Oil company workers also hunted them. Quickly the oryx vanished from much of its home range.

Naturalists realized that the animal would soon be extinct unless it was rescued quickly. In 1962, The Fauna

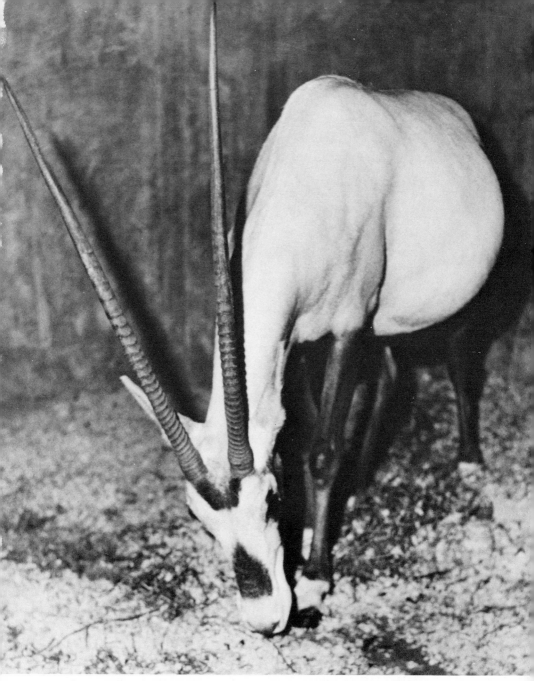

Oryx. This animal was in grave danger by the time a few
of them were caught and brought into captivity for a
breeding program.   COURTESY PHOENIX ZOO

Preservation Society sent out a party of wildlife workers to capture some of the last Arabian oryx. There seemed no way to save them from extinction except to keep them in captivity and hope they would reproduce. The project was called "Operation Oryx."

The leader was Major Ian Grimwood. From a small airplane he flew over the desert, searching for the last of the oryx. Finally he spotted two males and one female. These animals were captured safely, and they were soon taking a long airplane ride.

They were flown to Phoenix, Arizona. The money for their trip came from the World Wildlife Fund. In the Phoenix Zoo, the little herd has prospered.

The next year Major Grimwood located two Arab rulers who owned some oryx and wanted to send them to Phoenix to help save the species. American sportsmen, the American Arabian Oil Company, and many others cooperated to get these oryx to Arizona. Said Major Grimwood, writing in *Oryx,* the journal of the Fauna Preservation Society, ". . .this bodes well for further attempts which will almost certainly have to be made to save other vanishing species."

By 1968, the herd of oryx at the Phoenix Zoo contained ten males and six females. Other smaller herds were being started elsewhere. Meanwhile, in the wilds of Arabia, officials believe a small number still survive in the wild. These, however, are always in danger.

Operation Oryx has yet not ended. Hopefully, in some future year, wildlife biologists will find safe places where some of the captive animals may prosper again in the wild. Then they can be moved back to their native land. With all this work, and a lot of luck, the beautiful and graceful Arabian oryx may someday roam its native land once again, rescued from the threat of early extinction.

CHAPTER 10

Giant Tortoise

To visit the strange Galapagos Islands you must travel to Ecuador on the western coast of South America. Then you go westward by ship or aircraft for another 600 miles. You will travel along the Equator until the islands appear on the horizon.

A hundred years ago, if you had come to Santa Cruz Island, you might have seen a whaling ship riding at anchor in Academy Bay. For more than two years she might have been away from her home port, sailing the distant waters, searching for the giant whales.

Her captain did not put in at Academy Bay for whales, but to replenish the food supply. A crew would come ashore and, for the next four days, drive giant tortoises down from the hills and load them onto the ship.

Other whaling ships would come too, to capture and haul off more of the giant tortoises. During the months

Giant tortoise of the Galapagos Islands. The ancestors of these tortoises are believed to have come from the mainland of South America.

at sea the tortoises would provide fresh meat for the crews. One historian has studied the logs of some of these ships and found that 107 ships hauled off more than 15,000 Galapagos tortoises in thirty-three years during the early 1800s.

Some of the Galapagos Islands are tiny bits of lava scarcely rising above the sea. Others are larger ones up to seventy-five miles long. About 5,000 people live in these islands, most of them on just two of the islands. Each of the Galapagos Islands has its own mysteries. For many years naturalists have come here to study the strange plants and animals that are found nowhere else.

Most famous of all these naturalists was Charles Darwin, who arrived aboard the *Beagle* in 1835. Especially, he studied the native finches — the small sparrow-like birds that live only on these islands. He saw that the finches had evolved to fit the living conditions of the individual islands. Darwin's finches helped him understand the evolution of life and how species change and adapt to their surroundings.

Even more famous than the finches are the giant tortoises of the Galapagos. Around the world, millions of people who have never been to the Galapagos Islands have seen the giant tortoises in zoos. Scientists are concerned about tortoises, however, because they are threatened with extinction. There are several reasons.

Thousands were lost to the whalers. After the whalers came the settlers. On the larger islands they moved into the moist, high country. There they hacked farms out of the thick, jungle vegetation to grow coffee, bananas and grain. They also brought their own animals from the outside world. They brought to the Galapagos Islands the first goats, hogs, cats, dogs, donkeys and rats. The domestic animals were turned loose to find their own food.

Young tortoises became victims of rats, cats, dogs and swine. The eggs also were taken by hogs and rats.

In addition, there is the damage done by the goats. Few creatures anywhere are a greater threat to wildlife. Goats cause trouble by eating off the vegetation. As a result, the soil erodes and plants do not easily get a new start.

Still other tortoises were carried away from the islands by collectors. Some went for scientific studies, others to zoos and private collections. Several races of the Galapagos tortoises are already extinct. The others are in serious trouble.

How large is a Galapagos tortoise? Giants, they are called, and giants they are. Some have weighed five hundred pounds.

These reptiles evolved in a strange world. The Galapagos Islands have never been connected to the mainland. Instead, they rose from the ocean as molten lava. For hundreds of thousands of years the volcanoes continued to build the Galapagos Islands.

Plants may have come first on the feet of birds. Lizards rode floating logs. Winds carried seeds and insects. As for the tortoises, the ancestors of these Galapagos giants are believed to have come from the mainland of South America where their ancestors were much smaller.

But new islands can shape their own species. Over thousands of years, plants and animals change and adapt to new living conditions. Over the thousands of years, the tortoises became giants.

In addition, they developed different shapes on some of the islands than on others. The Galapagos tortoises

Giant tortoises were once taken from the Galapagos Islands in great numbers by whaling ships. Predators destroy the eggs.   COURTESY GEORGE LAYCOCK

are divided into two main groups. Some have shells with special saddles shaped in them above the animal's neck. These formations are like saddle horns and provide a notch into which the tortoise's neck can fit as it lifts its head high. Such tortoises evolved in the drier and lower islands where the tortoises feed on the tree cactus, which they must stretch their necks upward to reach.

Where there is lower-growing vegetation in the moist, high sections of the islands, the tortoises did not develop such shells. On Albemarle Island there are five ancient volcano craters. These volcanoes gradually grew together to form a single island. But each one had its own type of tortoise, each living nowhere else in the world except within its own volcanic crater.

These animals may live a hundred years or more, unless they slip over the edge of a cliff or tumble into a crevass from which they cannot escape.

The season of mating comes during the rainy weeks of March and April. These cumbersome creatures are slow travelers. But some of the females make surprisingly speedy trips down from the hills to the lowlands to lay their eggs. They come down in the dry season beginning in September, traveling perhaps three or four miles a day.

Each female will dig out a hole in the sand, drop into it perhaps ten to twenty white, leathery-shelled eggs and cover her treasure. Then she leaves the nesting area behind to start that long climb back up into the hills where she can find food. Meanwhile, the males have stayed behind in the hills, never returning to the lowlands where they hatched.

The eggs often are stolen by other animals. But scientists, working at the Charles Darwin Research Station at Academy Bay, have found a way to rescue the eggs. When I visited there, they took me to see their special incubators. The eggs of giant tortoises were being collected from the nests before the predators found them. After hatching, the young tortoises are kept until large enough to be safe, then taken to the hills and turned loose. In this way, men hope to save the threatened giants of the Galapagos Islands.

Today, the Przewalski horse is found in
several zoos where efforts are being
made to increase their numbers.
COURTESY CHICAGO ZOOLOGICAL
SOCIETY, BROOKFIELD ZOO

CHAPTER 11

The Wildest Horse

THE LITTLE BAND of horses in the vast Gobi Desert had probably never before seen a human being. The nine mares and colts were grazing in the open grassland, but the stallion, leader of the herd, was nervous by nature, constantly alert, and frequently lifted his head to inspect the surrounding countryside. Sometimes he stood for several minutes, watching. Then, satisfied, he would eat again.

Beyond the hill a famous explorer, traveling with a string of camels, led his party through the dry grasslands searching for any unusual wild animals he might encounter. He definitely did not expect to find wild horses. The ancient ancestors of the domesticated horse were believed to be extinct. The explorer was Colonel Nikolai Przewalski, a Russian naturalist. Many times he had traveled into this lonely part of Asia.

The movement of the plodding camels on the distant ridge brought the stallion's head up quickly. Every muscle in his powerful body was tensed. With a shrill warning to the mares and their colts, the old stallion put his herd in motion. The clatter of their hoofs beat upon the dry earth, and their long tails flared out behind them. The horses did not slow down until they were out of sight of the men and camels.

Colonel Przewalski, fascinated, watched the speeding horses vanish from sight. They were spirits of the wind, as wild in nature as any animals he had ever seen.

He noted their shape and color, and the difference between them and other kinds of horses. They were light yellowish brown. Their short manes stuck straight up above their necks.

Colonel Przewalski began talking with Mongolian herdsmen and searching for more of the strange horses. Within a few days he came upon another small herd that galloped off toward the horizon.

What the colonel had seen was the animal modern scientists believe to be the ancestor of domestic horses and ponies. They were creatures out of the Ice Age. Years later men would find cave paintings of such horses drawn by ancient, prehistoric artists. One cave in Lascaux, France, was discovered in 1940 by two boys hiking along a wooded hill. Their pet dog disappeared into a hole in the side of the hill. The boys followed.

There they discovered strange paintings on the walls, pictures mostly of large animals, bulls, deer and horses. There could be no doubt that such horses once lived in western Europe. In prehistoric times the horses were probably common.

Gradually, bits and pieces have been added to the story of this original wild horse. Its home now is in that vast, uninhabited semi-desert country along the border between Mongolia and the Chinese People's Republic. Its range stretches for about 200 miles from north to south and is as much as ninety miles across. In earlier times, herdsmen sometimes followed their grazing livestock into these wild places, but today even the herdsmen do not go there.

Where the wild horses might be depends on the season, the rains, and where there is grass for them. In some seasons they cross the border into China. They also wander into the grasslands of the Gobi Desert.

Sometimes people have seen one lone wild horse standing on a high ridge. These are most likely the males that do not belong to a herd. The strongest stallions drive the weak ones out.

In the summer of 1966, Dr. Zoltan Kaszab departed from his home in Budapest, Hungary, and his office in the Hungarian Natural History Museum. He had been asked to lead his fourth expedition into the dry wilderness country of western Mongolia.

Instead of using camels, Dr. Kaszab's party traveled in jeeps, and unlike Colonel Przewalski, the doctor knew what he was looking for. One day in the mountain country he saw a herd of horses galloping off at full speed. His Mongolian guides assured him that these were the Przewalski horses.

Soon his jeep was roaring across the grassland in pursuit. Dr. Kaszab studied the eight speeding horses through a telescope. He even took a few photographs with his unsteady camera. At twenty miles an hour, he followed for twenty minutes without reducing the distance.

Wherever men have settled, the wild horses have vanished until their range has shrunk to what it is today.

They have survived only in the loneliest outposts of their once broad range.

There is something about an untamed, wild horse that challenges men. Here is work undone. These powerful, snorting, wild-eyed monsters become a challenge, and man feels he must curb this defiant spirit and become the master. But the Przewalski horses refused to be captured.

At first, efforts were made to capture the mares and their young, but the mares would not be caught and subdued. If driven into pens, they fought until they died. Only by killing the females could their colts be captured. Between 1899 and 1902, perhaps fifty-four horses were brought into captivity.

Eventually the numbers in captivity increased. Careful records are kept on all of these animals to be certain that they are the pure-blooded horse. Today, there may be more of them in zoos than there are running wild over the dry hills of Mongolia where they have come to their last stand.

CHAPTER 12

A Giant Eagle

IN THE SOFT shadows of the mountain forest a huge bird sat silent and motionless on its favorite perch. Gradually the excited monkeys settled down and stopped screeching and scolding at it. The hornbills, with those threatening, thick bills, had also quieted and stopped trying to harass the great eagle. All the smaller woodland creatures now seemed to ignore the giant eagle whose large blue eyes studied every movement in the shadowy green forest.

Especially, the eagle watched a small flying lemur. The little mammal launched itself into the air and glided toward another tree nearby. And as it did, the old eagle silently pushed away from its perch.

On whispering wings, spanning ten feet of the forest shadows, the giant bird maneuvered through the trees, aiming at the point where the lemur would land. The lemur had not known that the eagle watched. Before it

The monkey-eating eagle, among the largest in the world, numbers fewer than 100 alive today.

sensed what was happening, the powerful bird made its capture. The monkey-eating eagle knew no other way of life. His role in the natural world is that of the predator. But not many of his kind are left, and conservationists believe that the monkey-eating eagle may soon be extinct. Perhaps fewer than 100 are still alive.

These are among the largest eagles in the world. Their powerful yellow feet carry black, inch-long talons, curved and needle-sharp. They are equipped with a thick, curved blue-gray bill. Around its head the monkey-eating eagle wears an arrangement of feathers which can flare up into a fluffy war bonnet whenever the eagle becomes excited.

These eagles are found living wild nowhere but in the Philippine Islands. They once lived on at least four islands there. Today they live on the island of Mindanao, and perhaps a few survive on Luzon.

The female lays only one egg, and she and her mate must incubate it for nearly two months before they learn whether or not it will hatch. Both parents work to incubate the egg and later to feed the downy, white young. For fifteen weeks, the young monkey-eating eagle stays in the nest while the old birds carry food to it, mostly young monkeys, flying lemurs, or birds.

What has brought this famous national bird of the Philippines to the brink of extinction? For one thing, people have moved into the forests where it lives. Also, these spectacular big birds are tempting targets for gunners. After World War II, there were many more guns in the Philippines than before.

There are laws to protect the monkey-eating eagle. But to do their job, laws must be enforced, and the shooting has gone on. Some people shoot monkey-eating eagles just to possess a stuffed trophy, a dead mass of

feathers held together by thread and decorated with two unblinking glass eyes.

There is still another reason for the monkey-eating eagle's troubles. Zoos want the famous rare birds for their displays. Fortunately, however, many zoos will no longer buy or sell wild creatures that are threatened with extinction unless the sale is approved by their association.

The Philippine government still hopes to save the spectacular monkey-eating eagle. Perhaps education can stop the trophy hunting. Meanwhile the government tries to protect the eagle's woodland breeding areas.

Other kinds of eagles, elsewhere in the world, also face trouble. The sea eagles, living largely on fish, are confronted with constant threats. One in special trouble is a big brown eagle found in Spain and called The Spanish Imperial Eagle. There may now be no more than fifty pairs of these eagles remaining.

In North America, the Bald Eagle, national bird of the United States, is in serious trouble. Originally the bald eagles lived over much of the North American Continent. Then men moved into their territories. They cut down the forests in which the eagles nested. Sheepmen, believing that eagles carry off lambs, waged ceaseless war against them. Some ranchers have sent hunters in helicopters to shoot hundreds of eagles out of the skies.

But the most serious of all the eagle's enemies is DDT, a chemical they cannot escape. This chemical came into

◀ The southern race of the bald eagle, national bird of the United States of America, is in danger of extinction.
COURTESY GEORGE LAYCOCK

wide use as a poison to kill insects shortly after World War II. Nobody knew what troubles it would bring to the ecosystems. It began to float in the air and water and moved through the food chains of the world.

DDT, and chemicals formed from it, cause eagles and other birds of prey to lay eggs with shells so thin that they are crushed in the nests. Such chemicals can also kill the young in the eggs even if the shells do not break. As a result, the bald eagle has vanished from state after state. Suddenly they are gone. Only in Florida and Alaska do sizable populations remain. There are smaller numbers in Minnesota, Wisconsin and parts of Canada.

Whether they live on monkeys and lemurs in the Philippines, rabbits in the marshes of Spain, or fish along the waters of North America, the world's eagles, these giants of the skies, face an uncertain future.

CHAPTER 13

The American Cougar

WHEN THE SHADOWS of darkness are filtering into the eastern forest, the silent creatures of the night leave their beds to move along the game trails. Graceful white-tailed deer move slowly toward the wild gardens where they gather leaves, buds and fruits. Owls float on ghostly wings through the night.

But some of the wild ones have nearly vanished from our eastern forests. These forests were once home to one of the world's most remarkable large cats, called the cougar, panther or mountain lion.

When the deer joined the animals of the night, the cougar was there as well. He might be eight feet long from the tip of his nose to the tip of his tail. He was a wild hunter which moved on whispering feet.

Gently he shifted his weight to each advancing foot, inching forward, crouching against the earth until the

A closeup portrait of the North American mountain lion, known also as the cougar, panther or puma.

fur of his belly slid across the ground. Before him, the feeding doe might lift her head every few bites. She would inspect the night, and her long, cupped ears would gather in the sounds.

Perhaps only one time out of three the giant cat would be successful on such a stalk. Between times, if forced to do so, he could turn to smaller game, rabbits, wild turkeys, even a porcupine if his gnawing hunger drove him to it.

The cougar evolved at the top of the food chain and, under natural conditions, played its vital role in the drama between predator and prey. Although the deer have come back and there are now hundreds of thousands of them, the cougar through most of its eastern range is gone, perhaps for all time.

Without question, the cougar once covered a greater range than any other New World mammal. Its original range extended from northern British Columbia eastward through Canada to the Atlantic Ocean. Southward, it was found through all of North America, Central America and South America down to Tierra del Fuego. Those living near the tropics are smaller, and somewhat lighter in color, than those in the northern sections of their range.

From sea level to mountain elevations of 10,000 feet, the cougar was at home. Some lived in the forests, some in the alpine meadows, some in the dry desert country. But they were never abundant. Each of these great cats must stake out for himself a hunting territory perhaps 15 miles across.

Into this wilderness scene came man to cut down the forests. His domestic animals lived in the fenced fields around his home. The land changed steadily. The wild creatures were in danger. This was true especially of the large animals whose nature seemed to conflict with the works of man.

With the forests and the deer disappearing, the cougar sometimes turned to calves and colts for food. For this reason, frontier settlers saw the cougar as an enemy to be destroyed. As early as 1764, Massachusetts placed a bounty on the cougar. Men hunted them with guns and dogs. They were believed extinct in Pennsylvania by 1891, and then were thought to be gone everywhere east of the Mississippi River except for a few hundred in northwestern Florida and in and around the Big Cypress Swamp. Meanwhile, the cougar seems to be returning to the northeastern United States, and it still lives in New Brunswick, Canada.

Today the eastern cougar has its name in the official Red Data Book of rare and endangered wildlife published by the International Union for Conservation of Nature and Natural Resources. There are broad, wild areas of South America where the cougar is as abundant as ever. And in some places in the western mountains of the United States they still hold forth in fair numbers.

What would a cougar look like if you were fortunate enough to see one? Their short hair is light brownish in color and their tails are long. Their legs are fairly short, and their feet broad for an animal of their size.

The male is larger than the female. He may weigh about 160 pounds while the female weighs about 135 pounds. The head is broad, the ears are short and rounded.

The female often has two or three furry little kittens hidden someplace beneath a tangle of brush or perhaps in a rocky cavern.

For the first ten days of their lives the kittens are blind and helpless. For six months their coats are spot-

Cougar kittens usually number two or three to the litter.
COURTESY KARL H. MASLOWSKI

ted. When they are about two months old, the mother takes them along on their first hunting trip. Their training begins.

Deer hunters sometimes dislike cougars because the big cats kill deer. But research has shown that the cougar catches the deer that are easiest to catch. In this way they often remove the weak and the diseased deer, and their hunting helps to keep the herds healthy and vigorous.

How many deer will a cougar kill in a year? Naturalists say about one a week. The cougar does not waste much food, but covers what is left, then returns on another night to feed on the leftovers.

The cougar is an elusive creature, a mystery animal. Often people report seeing them streak across the road at night, or tell of hearing their unearthly screams. Usually this is imagination. There may not be a wild, free-roaming cougar within a thousand miles. The thought of one wild in the neighborhood makes the heart beat faster.

Unfortunately, the chance that one of these American mountain lions is nearby is slight today. Like so many others, especially the large predators, the cougar is listed as a disappearing creature.

◀ A large cougar is effectively camouflaged in a snow-covered treetop in the mountains.   COURTESY U.S. BUREAU OF SPORT FISHERIES AND WILDLIFE

Komodo dragon. The Komodo monitors
are endangered because farmers kill them
to protect stock, and poachers kill their
prey. COURTESY NATIONAL
ZOOLOGICAL PARK

CHAPTER 14

Dragons

THE BODY OF a wild deer lay where the animal had fallen by the edge of the woods, and for two days the sun warmed the carcass. The strong odors were beginning to draw the big lizards out of the shadows. One giant scaly creature appeared from the edge of the forest.

It stood there on short, heavy legs, its beady little eyes scanning the scene. A long, forked tongue darted in and out of its wide mouth.

The huge reptile was nearly nine feet in length, had long, sharp claws and a wrinkled, leathery body narrowing to a long, thick tail. Its beady black eyes were set in a broad, flat head. The whole body was covered with a coat of tough, bony scales.

When it walked, it lifted its body a few inches off the ground. Its powerful tail dragged behind it, marking a line in the earth between the prints of its broad feet.

75

The dinosaur-like reptile stood with one big foot on the shoulder of the dead deer. Then, using its sharp claws, it dug into the flesh and ripped away large chunks. It gulped the food down, swallowing meat, bones, hair and all.

In addition to eating carrion, these animals, the Komodo Dragons, or monitor lizards, also capture live prey. They have been known to kill animals as large as water buffalo by first cutting the tendons in the hind legs. Having killed an animal, the giant Komodo monitor lizard may drag it off into the brush or tall grass.

Today, this ancient creature, after uncounted millions of years on earth, is low enough in numbers that conservationists watch it closely, seeking ways to help it survive.

Scientists believe the Komodo monitor may have descended from extinct giant monitors that lived in India many millions of years ago. The species may be older than the islands on which they live today. According to the records of the International Union for Conservation of Nature, perhaps only 400 breeding female Komodo monitors still live. There are many more males than females.

Home to the Komodo dragon is on a few islands in Indonesia: Komodo, Rintja, Padar, and a portion of Flores. These lie in the Lower Sundas group of islands. The largest number live on the 22-mile-long Komodo Island where volcanic peaks rise to more than 2,000 feet above sea level. On such islands thousands of years of erosion have cut the lava and volcanic ash into sharp-walled valleys. Some of Komodo's slopes are blanketed with verdant jungles of thick-growing shrubs, trees, and vines. Some areas are grasslands.

Within the thickets, the Komodo dragon digs its

caves, hides and hunts for food. The females lay their eggs in the earth. The newly hatched baby monitors are slender, and their bodies are about twenty inches long, with heavy yellowish markings. From the hour they hatch, they are able to rush about the ground or climb onto the limbs of the trees. The young spend much of their time in trees to escape the older ones, which would eat them.

Why did the world go so long without hearing about these giant lizards? For one reason, its islands were seldom visited by outsiders. Only an occasional visiting fisherman went there and he would not stay long.

But these fishermen began telling of the strange creatures they had seen on Komodo. Back in the city now known as Bogor, Java, the director of the museum there was Major P.A. Ouwens. He was curious about the unusual stories and wanted them to be investigated.

This led to a small expedition being sent to Komodo, and scientific workers viewed, for the first time, the giant monitor lizards which were to become known as the "Komodo Dragons." One skin which Major Ouwens measured was said to be thirteen feet long. The Komodo dragon, however, seldom grows longer than nine feet.

Following his investigations, Major Ouwens wrote a report of his discovery, and soon scientists around the world knew there were giant lizards living on the islands. Other scientists went seeking them. Some went only to capture the lizards for zoos. There are now perhaps fourteen Komodo dragons in zoos around the world. In only one or two instances have they reproduced in captivity.

The native people of Indonesia do not kill many of the big lizards. One reason is the law which the Indonesian government passed, making it illegal to capture or harm this rare animal.

In addition, Padar and Rintja are sanctuaries. Scientists have recommended that part of Komodo Island also be set aside as a refuge for the lizards. Farmers on Flores put out poison to kill the giant lizards, claiming that the Komodo monitor eats farm animals.

The biggest threat to the Komodo dragon may be goats. Around the world, goats have destroyed large areas wherever men have taken them, especially on islands. They ruin the brush and native plants, leaving the soil open to erosion. On Komodo, goats are destroying the vegetation on which the deer and wild hogs live, and these are the animals which provide a good supply of food for the strange dragons of Komodo.

In addition to poisoning, a big threat to the Komodo dragon is deer poaching. The poachers, who take hundreds of deer, deprive the monitors of their food supply. Burning of the natural vegetation by people of the islands is another source of trouble for the lizards. Such ecological changes, especially on small islands, can be disastrous to the native wildlife. The huge reptiles' numbers are low and their future is bleak.

CHAPTER 15

Parrots of
Puerto Rico

THEY FLEW ACROSS the steep-walled valley like a green cloud, chattering and squawking to each other as they moved. Many years earlier, explorers had heard the voices of the parrots as their ships approached the island. The birds lived there by the thousands. They perched in the trees, ate the fruit and buds and filled the forests with their calls.

Those were good times for the parrots of Puerto Rico. But now they may soon be extinct.

When a flock of Puerto Rican parrots comes into a tree to eat, they crawl around over the limbs, sometimes hanging upside down. Meanwhile, there is one that does not eat. Instead, it has stationed itself in the top of the tree, standing guard. If hawk, cat or man appears, the bird on guard sounds the alarm and the parrots leave the tree, like a handful of green feathers on the wind.

Museum specimen of the Carolina parakeet, a member of the parrot family, already extinct.

Their small cousins, the Carolina parakeets, once lived on the North American Continent. But they fed in gardens and fruit orchards. Farmers shot thousands of the Carolina parakeets. The last one died in the Cincinnati Zoo in 1918.

Unless something can be done quickly to save them, the last of the Puerto Rican parrots also will be gone.

Before the settlers came to Puerto Rico, the island was almost completely covered with timber. Then the forests were cut for lumber and charcoal. More trees were cleared also, to make space for growing crops. Finally, only in the high rain forests could the parrots find the safety and food they required for survival.

They are making their final stand on only a fraction of their original range in the eastern part of their island. There the last of them live at elevations between 1600 and 2700 feet above sea level, in the wet tropical forests, within the Caribbean National Forest. It is there, in an experimental forest named Loquillo, that the parrots have found their last refuge.

In addition, two of them lived for several years in a zoo at Mayaguez. Their keeper always hoped they would nest and raise young. But they never made any efforts to mate.

Eventually these two parrots were shipped off to Maryland to be cared for and studied by biologists of the U.S. Bureau of Sport Fisheries and Wildlife. I visited them there one day. They lived in a large wire-enclosed room and spent much of their time flying from one wall to the other, clinging to the wire with their feet. They are beautiful birds, brilliant light green in color with dark blue markings on the long primary feathers of their wings, and red marks across the fronts of their faces. They may have measured a foot in length from the tips

of their thick, curved bills to the tips of their stubby, green tails.

Why had these birds never mated and nested? The males and females look exactly alike, and biologists now believe that both are females. From the forests of Puerto Rico may come mates for them. Hopefully, they can still raise young which may someday be taken back for release in Puerto Rico.

To figure out how such a plan might best succeed, the United States sent ornithologist Dr. Cameron B. Kepler to Puerto Rico to study the parrots. Dr. Kepler became the world's leading authority on the habits of these parrots.

First, he wanted to know how many were left. By using his knowledge of the mountains, he marked out twelve straight lines on his maps. Each of these was one kilometer (six-tenths of a mile) long. And each went through territory where the parrots were believed to live.

Then he began a series of hikes along these rugged census routes. Each route was walked every two months by Dr. Kepler and his wife. For the scientists there must be order in such a search. He must test the same areas at regular intervals and check them in the same manner and at similar times. In this way, after enough trips along his census routes, Dr. Kepler could begin to un-

Puerto Rican parrot, a bright green bird and one of the rarest of the endangered species, is native to Puerto Rico and confined to Luquillo National Forest.
COURTESY LUTHER C. GOLDMAN
U.S. BUREAU OF SPORT FISHERIES
AND WILDLIFE

derstand whether he was still finding parrots where they had been before, and whether their numbers were changing. With his notebook in hand, and his binoculars hanging from his neck, Dr. Kepler recorded every parrot seen or heard.

"Much of my time," he wrote in one government report, "is spent in unsuccessful searches for parrots."

Part of the time he studied the pearly-eyed thrashers, similar to the brown thrashers of North America. In addition to its diet of fruits and insects, this bird kills and eats young birds of other species. The numbers of the pearly-eyed thrasher have increased greatly in recent years, although no one can be quite certain why this has happened. As the number of thrashers increased, the parrots decreased. Biologists believe the thrashers may be competing with parrots for the nesting cavities in hollow trees. In addition, rats, which are abundant in the forests of Puerto Rico, will eat the parrot eggs and young.

Back in the Patuxent Wildlife Research Center, in Maryland, biologists are devising a plan to save the Puerto Rican parrot. Here is how such a system may work, if the captive birds nest and produce young.

These infant parrots will grow up in a parrot house where they will never see the men who work with them. Food and water will be given to them through chutes and pipes. If they see no human beings, they will not learn that man provides them with safety and food. After several years, when they are mature and ready to reproduce, they can be transported, still in boxes hidden from view, back to the home forests of their ancestors and set free.

Something has to be done about providing them with nesting places. Artificial nest boxes will be waiting for the young birds in their native forests. These will be designed for parrots and made so that rats and thrashers cannot easily enter them.

This plan may or may not succeed. Years may pass before we know whether the Puerto Rican parrot has come down to the finish line.

The cheetah is threatened because of habitat destruction, poaching and killing by livestock owners.
COURTESY ERWIN A. BAUER

CHAPTER 16

The Speeding Cheetah

THE HUNT BEGINS with the lithe form of the great cat crouched low in the grass, blending into the sun-dappled pattern. Like a statue, the cheetah waits and watches the sleek, brown impala as they feed. The impala move gradually along, nearer, unaware that an ancient enemy waits in the shadows. Seventy-five yards. Sixty yards. Fifty yards.

But the impala turn away to the right. The hunting cat knows it must make its move while there is time. He inches forward, shortening the distance between himself and the impala.

At the edge of the tall grass, the cheetah heaves his body forward, gaining speed from the strength of his long, powerful legs. Quickly the cheetah has closed the first twenty feet of the distance, but at this instant the impala, in a single moment of panic, have bounded with

high, arching leaps up and over the grass in beautiful, soaring broad jumps.

But here the cheetah is at his best. If he is to make the kill, it must be accomplished in those first few minutes. He is not a distance runner, but on the short dash he can run at speeds well over a mile a minute. The world's fastest race horse would run in the cheetah's dust, because this big cat is the fastest of all land mammals. One cheetah was clocked at 71 miles an hour, a speed the graceful cat can keep up for a couple of hundred yards. But after that, the impala begin to stretch the distance between them, and the cheetah must start over again.

One of the impala, however, perhaps a young one, or an old or injured one, may falter. The change is noted instantly by the dashing cheetah. He alters his course slightly and puts his entire attention on the single animal. In the following instant the impala is brought to the ground, while the rest of the herd bounds off and out of sight.

This scene is one that is becoming increasingly rare throughout the range of the cheetah, because the world's speediest runner is vanishing. There was a time when the cheetah lived across Africa, except in its rain forests and the deserts, and also across much of southern Asia.

If you study the cheetah closely, you soon begin to learn that it is unlike all of the other large, spotted cats. Instead of hunting at night, it is abroad in the daytime.

In a short dash, the cheetah is the fastest mammal in the world. One cheetah was clocked at 71 miles per hour!
COURTESY KARL H. MASLOWSKI

In some ways it resembles a dog as much as a cat. Its manner of running its prey is doglike, and it is the only one of the big cats that does not possess retractable claws.

The cheetah does not grow especially big, seldom more than 115 pounds. It has a long and slender body, and a head that seems small in proportion to its size.

Its diet may include such birds as guinea fowl and francolins, hares and other small creatures, a total of about twenty-five species. But such animals as the impala, gazelle and waterbuck, make up a large percentage of its kills.

Men have taken many cheetahs captive. But more important, they have destroyed the habitat of both the cheetahs and the wild prey that provides their food.

In addition, people still try to obtain cheetahs for pets. There are pet cheetahs today in apartments in the United States as well as other places around the world.

In some African countries the laws permit the killing of cheetahs if they are believed to be a threat to livestock. Having killed the animal, the farmer is permitted to sell its extremely valuable fur. Under such circumstances it becomes easy to convince oneself that cheetahs may be threatening the goats and sheep even when the cheetahs are many miles away. Then the fur goes to the big city to become a spotted coat for some lady.

In man the cheetah met a predator that is destroying him. The cheetah kills to survive, and takes what he needs to eat. Man kills cheetahs for lesser reasons.

How many cheetahs are there? In all of Africa there may be no more than 2,000 remaining. Each year there appear to be fewer than the year before. Across hundreds of square miles where the cheetah once hunted, the big spotted cats are now gone, perhaps forever.

CHAPTER 17

The White Bears

BY EARLY OCTOBER, the days were growing steadily darker beyond the Arctic Circle, and the old white bear moved inland away from the sea. The world was white with fresh snow and she was headed toward her denning area. She came eventually to the mouth of the long valley where she had denned up for the winter two years before.

She stopped frequently and looked around her as she continued to move up the side of the hill. The restless, howling wind carried snow off the plains above and out over the valley to fall in a deep bank along the side of the hill. The old bear started to work.

When she finished, she had dug a den in the snowbank big enough for her massive body. She crawled at last to the back of the den, curled up, and rested her long snout on her front paws. Full darkness was settling over the world. The wind sounds were quieter, and in-

The adult polar bear has few enemies except man.
COURTESY GEORGE LAYCOCK

side the bear's den, it was very soon snug and warm.

Through those first weeks of the long winter she lay curled snugly in her darkened snow cave. She was not in true hibernation, but only in a deep sleep. Now the cave was about to become the nursery for her two un-born cubs, and she enlarged the shelter to make room for them.

When they were born, the two baby polar bears were helpless and nearly naked, but they found warmth by snuggling into the long, white fur that covered their mother's body. They were exceedingly small for a mother so large. Each one weighed about one and a half pounds. In the days that followed, the tiny bears knew the warmth of their mother's fur around them and the wonderful taste of the warm, thick milk she gave them hour after hour. When the spring sun began to weaken the roof of her shelter, growing pangs of hunger were felt in her rum-bling belly. The old sow bear came out and brought her new white cubs for their first look at the outdoors.

Not all the polar bears, however, had denned up for the winter. The males and young unbred females had wandered through the bitter Arctic winter hunting and denning up only in the worst storms. Mostly, polar bears are meat eaters. Seals are a favorite food. But when the ice is gone during the brief Arctic summer and the seals are difficult to catch, the bears settle for berries, roots, lichens and whatever small creatures they can capture.

By early autumn the white bears are eating heavily and laying on layers of fat to help them through the approaching winter.

During their second summer the young will separate from their mother. Now they must go off to make their own way in the world.

These white bears are among the largest of the world's

Even in the remote Arctic, the great white bears were not safe once hunters began using airplanes.

COURTESY JACK LENTFER
ALASKA DEPARTMENT OF FISH AND GAME

CHAPTER 18

The Vanishing King of Beasts

WHERE THE LITTLE pride of lions loaf in the dappled shadows of the scrub growth, there is a quiet sleepiness over the region. The lions have rested for many hours. Late in the day they begin to stir and stretch.

The three cubs begin to chase each other and tumble recklessly over the older lions. Slowly the old male stands.

His muscular body measures nearly nine feet from his nose to the bush on the tip of his tail. He weighs nearly 400 pounds and stands three feet high at the shoulders. His fur is smooth and tawny. His broad head, with its powerful jaws, is framed in a shaggy mane of long hair.

The females do most of the hunting and killing. In some prides there are more than one male and several females, as well as the younger animals, perhaps ten to twenty lions living in one group.

Lions in the Gir Forest, India. These remarkable, big cats are gradually dwindling.   COURTESY ERWIN A. BAUER

The female is considerably smaller than her mate. Rising from her resting place in the scrubby thicket, she is a slender, powerfully built cat with strong legs and large claws on her broad feet.

The range of the lions once stretched across Africa and Asia and even much of southern Europe. But men and lions were always enemies, because men said it was so. Ancient kings and noblemen hunted with spears and arrows and made fantastic claims of killing large numbers of lions. The king of beasts was killed for the challenge and the glory of the hunt. Meanwhile, wild creatures on which they fed were gradually replaced by the herdsman's cattle and goats.

By A.D. 100, the lions were gone from all of Europe. By 1900, they were gone also from North Africa and from Southeast Asia.

In Africa, only the lions south of the Sahara remained in any numbers. The subspecies that had occupied the wild places across Asia were all gone except for a little group of thirteen. These clung to life in the Kathiawar Peninsula on the northwestern coast of India.

This Asian lion was on the fragile edge of extinction. Men had whittled away its world and reduced its numbers to one final baker's dozen, a remnant population that could vanish at any time.

Then the Indian government decided to save the last of its lions. Perhaps tourists would travel long distances just to see a wild lion.

To accomplish this, the government operates the Gir Sanctuary. At first the 483 thousand square miles of the Gir Forest were set aside. It is a strange sanctuary where unusual episodes occur.

Protection brought the lion numbers back to 250 by

Lions once occupied a range far wider than they do today.
COURTESY SOUTH AFRICAN TOURIST
CORPORATION, PRETORIA

1950. Since then the numbers have fallen again. Today there are perhaps only 175 wild Asian lions.

There could be more except that the Gir Forest area is also home to seven thousand people and more than fifty thousand head of domestic livestock. The buffalo, antelope and other wild creatures have been replaced by cattle.

What does a lion do when his natural source of food is eliminated? He turns to what he can still catch. If cattle is all he can find, beefsteak will do. So the little groups of lions, the last of the Asian subspecies, survive by killing the cattle that belong to the people.

On the hunt, the pride, as a group of lions living together is called, may follow the female out of the resting place like shadows slipping through the thicket. They hunt carefully and quietly and know how to ambush their prey. As they approach the grazing animals, the female crouches close against the earth.

This is no time to hurry. Stealth and patience count. The herd wanders slowly toward the clump of brush where she hides. She waits, her eyes never leaving the cattle. She is ready for that first, violent surge of power. At top speed, and for a short distance, the adult lion can run at sixty miles an hour.

She now studies one of the cattle, perhaps a scrawny, reddish-brown creature moving from plant to plant and wandering farther from the main herd. Then she comes bounding out of the shadows. The powerful lioness covers the distance quickly, hits the prey and brings it to earth as the remainder of the herd panics and scatters.

To the lions, who gather quickly around the kill, this hunt is essential to life. But to the people the loss of a cow is a burden.

This is the conflict between people and lions in the Gir Sanctuary. People will win out.

There is another serious threat to the Asian lions. This was discovered by a research biologist, Paul Joslin, when he went out from Edinburgh University in Scotland to study the last of the lions.

He told of the people who sell cowhides and the strange way they obtain these hides. They watch and wait for the lions to start off on a hunt. While the lions stalk their prey, the people hang back and wait. Then, with much yelling, the tribesmen rush forward and chase the lions from their kill before the hides are torn up.

While the hungry lions wait in the shadows, the hide hunters skin out the newly killed cow. Even after the men depart, the lions stay back, afraid to return to the kill for perhaps an hour or longer. By that time there is little left. The vultures have settled to earth and taken the meat.

What can be done to save the dwindling population of Asian lions? They may not be saved in the wild at all. They may be caught and kept behind high fences where each pride will have a few acres of its own. "One solution," Paul Joslin has said, "is to transplant the lions to another area. But where?" Some are now being taken to a new place in India by the IUCN working with a group of hunters. Someday, their descendants may be returned to live in the Gir Forest.

Around the world today the story is the same. Hundreds of wild species move steadily closer to the end of their time.

Men work to rescue the endangered ones. We have brought the pronghorn antelope of the western plains back from the edge of extinction. We have likewise rescued the trumpeter swans, and saved the bison. Even the whooping cranes, rare as they are, are slowly building up their numbers under man's protection.

As long as a few individuals of a species remain alive there is hope that their kind can be saved. If this fails, another wild species is lost forever.

Some Other
Endangered Wildlife

MAMMALS

LEADBEATER'S OPOSSUM   *Gymnobelideus leadbeateri*
This marsupial animal was once widely distributed over Victoria, Australia. For many years it was believed to have become extinct. Then, in 1961, it was rediscovered. Man is not blamed for the plight of this animal. Instead, scientists believe that gradual changes in climate brought changes in the vegetation to which the creature could not easily adjust. Refuge land has been set aside for its protection.

AYE-AYE   *Daubentonia madagascariensis*
This strange little primate is a forest animal, about the size of a house cat, and native to Madagascar. It is considered one of the rarest mammals in the world. Why? Forests where the animal evolved are being destroyed. It is also a victim of superstition. The appearance of an

Black-footed ferret, one of the rare and endangered species now under study. This alert ferret is looking over the prairie dog town where it lives.

COURTESY LUTHER C. GOLDMAN
U.S. BUREAU OF SPORT FISHERIES AND WILDLIFE

aye-aye in a village is considered a warning of death, and the only known method of saving the doomed people, so the villagers believe, is to kill the animal. Efforts are being made to save them on a small island refuge where the coastal forests still stand.

GOLDEN LION MARMOSET   *Leontideus rosalia*
    This rare and beautiful creature is a primate that survives only in a small section of rain forest in southeastern Brazil. The golden lion marmoset, wearing a coat of spectacular yellow, is almost extinct. In its native territory, forests fell and villages rose, as men moved in. Its range continues to shrink. There are about eighty of them in zoos where efforts are being made to raise them.

SNUB-NOSED MONKEY   *Rhinopithecus roxellanae*
    This beautiful, large monkey lives on a diet of leaves in the high, cold mountains of western China and eastern Tibet. In the past, its fur was highly prized. Some people even believed that by wearing the fur of this monkey they could cure their rheumatism. Now these monkeys are completely protected by law, but there are still reports of their fur showing up in shops. No one knows how many are left.

ORANGUTAN   *Pongo pygmaeus*
    See text pages.

GIANT ANTEATER   *Myrmecophaga tridactyla*
    Through much of its grassland range, the giant anteater of South America has become rare. Its greatest promise of safety lies now in national parks and refuges. Many anteaters have been killed by people, in spite of the fact that this slow-moving, harmless animal is seldom used for food and has a skin of almost no value.

Nobody knows how many of them survive. The possibilities of breeding them in zoos are remote.

BRAZILAN THREE-TOED SLOTH   *Bradypus torquatus*

This slow, leaf-eating mammal spends much of its time hanging upside down in the trees. It lives on leaves, twigs, and buds. The hair of the sloth lies in the opposite direction from that of most mammals. This allows the rain to run off his body quickly as the sloth hangs upside down.

GIANT ARMADILLO   *Priodontes giganteus*

This is a large, armored creature at home in the forests of South America. The adult may weigh 100 pounds and measure four feet in length. Its body is covered with heavy armor. On its front feet it has the largest claws of any animal and uses this equipment to tear apart rotten logs and anthills where it finds much of its food. Nobody knows how many of these remarkable animals remain. In the past they have been killed for human food. The cutting of the forest and the turning of the fields to agricultural crops have cut heavily into the number of giant armadillos.

KAIBAB SQUIRREL   *Sciurus kaibabensis*

There are perhaps 1,000 individuals remaining of this little squirrel. It is a native of the Kaibab Plateau on the northern side of the Grand Canyon in Arizona. This squirrel is found only where there are yellow pines because its primary food is the cambium layer of this tree. Because of its restricted range and its low numbers, it is on the list of rare and endangered species.

DELMARVA PENINSULA FOX SQUIRREL
Sciurus niger cinereus

This large, handsome, grayish-colored fox squirrel is

Grizzly bears have vanished from much of their original range in North America. COURTESY ERWIN A. BAUER

found in only six counties of eastern Maryland. At one time, years ago, it lived over a much wider area along the eastern shore. Its habitat has been gradually reduced, and it faces a dim future in spite of efforts to protect its habitat in wildlife refuges and state forests.

BLACK-TAILED PRAIRIE DOG   *Cynomys ludovicianus*
Man, advancing across the western range with his livestock, considered the prairie dog a competitor. Poisons have been used against it for many years. The black-tailed prairie dog is already extinct in many areas where it was once abundant. Endangered along with it are the black-footed ferrets and the burrowing owls which are all part of the same ecosystem. The white-tailed prairie dog is more numerous.

VICUNA   *Vicugna vicugna*
See text pages.

CHINCHILLA   *Chinchilla laniger*
This little South American mammal wears rich, thick fur that is the envy of people. This is bad for the chinchilla. It was widely distributed throughout the Andes. It is now believed extinct in Peru and rare in other countries through its range. It is now protected by law. Chinchillas are often raised in captivity, especially on fur farms.

RED WOLF   *Canis niger*
The red wolf once ranged across the southern United States from Florida to central Texas. Today it is found, in remnant numbers, in only a few areas. No one knows how many pure-blooded red wolves remain. It has been hunted, its habitat has been destroyed, and it has hybridized with coyotes which have increased in the range of the red wolf. This hybridization threatens to eliminate

Leopards, such as this one in Tanzania, like large cats almost everywhere, are seriously threatened.
COURTESY ERWIN A. BAUER

the last of the pure-blooded red wolves. Possibly the red wolf can be preserved in captivity and on a few wildlife refuges.

BLACK-FOOTED FERRET   *Mustela nigripes*

The black-footed ferret today is one of the rarest of all North America's mammals. The best possibility of saving them from extinction appears to be in the preservation of prairie dog towns, where they are still found, particularly in the Dakotas. As man wiped out the prairie dog towns, he also made it impossible for the black-footed ferret to survive because the ferret depends upon the prairie dog for prey.

MANED WOLF   *Chrysocyon brachyurus*

This large wild dog of South America has remarkably long legs and can run at high speeds. It does most of its hunting at night through the mixed forest and open areas. Like many other wild creatures, the maned wolves have been victims of man's spreading civilization. Their forest homes have been destroyed, and mounted horsemen run them down and kill them.

BUSH DOG   *Speothos venaticus*

This little brownish-colored, short-legged wild dog of South American forests runs in packs and hunts at night. There is not much known about this elusive species except that it is generally rare. Sometimes Brazilian people catch bush dogs and keep them as pets.

GIANT PANDA   *Ailuropoda melanoleuca*

See text pages.

SPECTACLED BEAR   *Tremarctos ornatus*

The only bear native to the Southern Hemisphere is the rare spectacled bear. This little bear stands only slightly more than two feet high at the shoulder. It is an elusive animal of the forest. As its native forests have been cut, its numbers have fallen. There are some in zoos around the world, and zoologists believe that they can be successfully reared.

MEXICAN GRIZZLY BEAR   *Ursus horribilis nelsoni*

This race of grizzly bear is in grave danger. Man has shot them relentlessly, and stockmen have poisoned them. Laws to protect them in Mexico have been poorly enforced. Meanwhile, the bear's cousin, the barren-ground grizzly of the Arctic, is also in serious difficulty. On the open tundra they are easily seen at great distances. And too often, whenever spotted by man, they are in danger, in spite of laws passed to protect them.

POLAR BEAR   *Thalarctos maritimus*

See text pages.

SOUTHERN SEA OTTER   *Enhydra lutris nereis*

In prehistoric times, the sea otter lived at the edge of the ocean from the stormy Aleutian Islands down the coast to southern California. Discovered in 1841 by Russian explorers, the sea otter was immediately popular with fur hunters. It wears a fabulously rich fur coat. In succeeding years, the Russians, followed by the Americans, took the sea otters as fast as they could. They eliminated total populations until it was believed the sea otter was extinct. However, remnant numbers remained. One of these little reservoirs was in the Aleutian Islands where the sea otter has since prospered under full protection. Meanwhile, the southern race of sea otters survived in small numbers off the coast of California where it still lives in a small and threatened population. Sea otters are fully protected by law and carefully watched by conservationists. But they are still threatened by water pollution, especially oil spills, and also are in danger of being shot by abalone fishermen.

AMERICAN COUGAR   *Felis concolor*
See text pages.

BARBARY SERVAL   *Felis serval constantina*
This extremely rare wildcat of north Africa has a body about three feet long, long legs, small head, and large ears. It is light brownish in color and marked with black spots. Most of its hunting is done at night for prey such as guinea fowl and small rodents. No one knows how many still survive, but it is believed to be one of the rarest mammals in north Africa.

CHEETAH   *Acinonyx jubatus*
See text pages.

AMUR LEOPARD   *Panthera pardus orientalis*
Leopards, like most of the large, spotted cats, are in serious trouble. This leopard has long been rare but is now almost extinct and living perhaps nowhere but in northern Korea. In 1970, only thirty or forty of them were estimated to still be living in the wild. They are protected by laws. Some are in zoos, and some have been born in captivity.

ASIATIC LION   *Panthera leo persica*
See text pages.

TIGER   *Panthera tigris*
See text pages.

CARIBBEAN MONK SEAL   *Monachus tropicalis*
The Caribbean Monk Seal is listed as "nearly extinct." In the past they have made little effort to es-

Monk seal, Hawaiian Islands, National Wildlife Refuge.
Twin pups are a rarity among seals.
COURTESY EUGENE KRIDLER
U.S. BUREAU OF SPORT FISHERIES AND WILDLIFE

cape as people closed in and killed them. Because of this, they have now been rare for more than a century. If some still survive, they come ashore only in remote hidden coves of seldom visited islands.

FLORIDA MANATEE   *Trichechus manatus latirostris*
This timid aquatic mammal looks like a big, shapeless leather bag. It sometimes reaches weights of 1,500 pounds. Its food consists of plants that grow in the shallow bays and sluggish coastal rivers. It may eat 100 pounds of vegetation in a day. Formerly, it was common all along the coast from North Carolina to Texas. Now, however, it is found only in restricted parts of Florida. In the past, it has been killed for its flesh, and because it tears up fishnets in which it becomes entangled. Its most important sanctuary is the Everglades National Park.

Elsewhere in the world, relatives of the Florida manatee are also in serious trouble. The Amazonian manatee may soon become extinct. One famous cousin of these animals which has already become extinct is Stellar's sea cow, discovered in 1841 in the Aleutian Islands, and extinct less than three decades later.

PYGMY HIPPOPOTAMUS   *Choeropsis liberiensis*
This little hog-sized hippopotamus is believed to be disappearing from the forests of Liberia and Sierra Leone as the forests are cut. Although the species is rare, it is not considered to be in immediate danger of extinction. Females mature at the age of eight years and ordinarily give birth to one young at a time. These animals are also hunted for food.

PRZEWALSKI HORSE   *Equus przewalskii*
See text pages.

The Key deer, the smallest race of the whitetail, is an endangered species of the Florida Keys.

COURTESY DONALD W. PFITZER
U.S. BUREAU OF SPORT FISHERIES AND WILDLIFE

PÈRE DAVID'S DEER   *Elaphurus davidianus*

This large deer, which stands 45 inches high at the shoulder, has only been saved in captive herds. Formerly its range stretched over a large part of eastern Asia. In 1865, a French missionary sent breeding stock of Père David's Deer to England where the Duke of Bedford established a herd. This was fortunate because in 1900 all of the remaining captive herd in China was destroyed. Since then, however, surplus deer from the Duke of Bedford's herd have been sent around the world and there are more than 500 of them.

KEY DEER   *Odocoileus virginianus clavium*

Hunting, development, fires, and highway deaths have reduced this smallest of all of the races of white-tailed deer to the endangered list. It lives only on the Florida Keys. There were probably no more than thirty by 1949. The Key deer was brought back from the edge of extinction by the U.S. Bureau of Sport Fisheries and Wildlife in the Key Deer National Wildlife Refuge. Today there are perhaps 600 of them. Most of those killed now die either on the highways or are dragged down by free-running dogs.

CHILEAN PUDU   *Pudu pudu*

This smallest deer in the Western Hemisphere is very rare but still found in the lower slopes of the Andes in Argentina and Chile. Forest fires, dogs, and hunters have reduced their numbers.

ASIATIC BUFFALO   *Bubalus bubalis*

These magnificent, powerful buffalo of the swamps of southern Asia and Borneo have been crowded out of much of their original range which is now under cultivation. Also, they have contracted diseases from domestic stock. Poachers still take them.

LOWLAND ANOA   *Anoa depressicornis depressicornis*

This midget of the cattle tribe is found now only in very small, restricted areas of wet forest in the Celebes. When fully grown, the Anoa bull stands about 40 inches at the shoulder. They are elusive forest creatures, and a source of meat for the people of their island. Until a few decades ago this little wild ox roamed a much wider area. Then forests were cut and fields put to crops for human food. As a result, the Anoa has been brought close to extinction.

SELADANG   *Bos gaurus hubaccki*

This animal, also known as the Gaur, is the largest of the wild cattle and lives in the forested mountains of southern Asia. The bull may stand more than six feet high at the shoulder. But wherever people have invaded its territory, the seladang has given way. In recent times, cultivation in particular has destroyed habitat, reducing constantly the areas where these remarkable wild cattle could live. The time may soon come when no wild ones remain. There are small numbers in zoos, and they have been successfully bred in captivity.

WILD YAK   *Bos grunniens mutus*

In the high, bitterly cold mountains of Tibet, the shaggy-coated yak has been a valuable domestic animal for many centuries. Throughout those years, however, the yak has still lived in the wild. Today these wild populations of yak have been reduced to a dangerous level. They have been relentlessly killed. In Tibet, the domesticated ones are used for riding, milking, and meat production.

BONTEBOK   *Damaliscus dorcas dorcas*

See text pages.

GIANT SABLE ANTELOPE   *Hippotragus niger variani*
This is a large antelope, native to the forests of south and east Africa. Bulls may weigh 500 pounds. Because the graceful horns of this animal may be more than five feet long, its head has been valued as a trophy. This has worked against its welfare. It has been wantonly shot by poachers. Unless the poaching stops and the animals are fully protected, there can be no hope for its future. No one knows how many of them still roam the forest.

ORYX   *Oryx leucoryx*
See text pages.

SWAYNE'S HARTEBEEST   *Alcelaphus buselaphus swaynei*
This is a large antelope, native to the plains of Africa. It may reach weights of 400 pounds. So fleet of foot is it that no other land animal with the exception of the cheetah can outrun it. Of the several races of hartebeest this subspecies is the form in greatest danger. Perhaps the first major enemy of this animal was a disease known as rinderpest in the 1890s. Added to that were losses from hunting.

BIRDS

GALAPAGOS PENGUIN   *Spheniscus mendiculus*
In prehistoric times this tiny penguin came north on the Humboldt Current to the Galapagos Islands. Today it still is found there, nesting among the lava rocks at the edge of the sea. In the past, hunters have taken these birds for food and also have collected their eggs.

Although their numbers are down and they are considered rare, they are probably holding their own at present.

GIANT PIED-BILLED GREBE   *Bodilymbus gigas*

This giant member of the grebe family is found nowhere in the world except on Lake Atitlan in Guatemala. Even there it has become very rare. Scientists consider it to be in grave danger of extinction. One of the big causes for the bird's problem seems to be that largemouth black bass were taken from the United States in 1957 and stocked in Lake Atitlan. These big fish eat the young grebes. Meanwhile, people continue to shoot the birds and take their eggs. There is also the problem of destroying habitat through the cutting of reeds along the shore.

EVERGLADE KITE   *Rostrhamus sociabilis plumbeus*

See text pages.

NEWELL'S MANX SHEARWATER

Puffinus puffinus newelli

This bird of the open sea comes ashore on the Hawaiian Islands to nest. A pair produces one egg and nests down at the end of a tunnel. One of their most important nesting areas is the island of Kauai, one of the Hawaiian Islands which does not have the imported mongoose. The mongooses, along with imported rats, cats, dogs, and pigs, make quick work of ground-nesting birds and their eggs. It is believed that the Shearwater is not immediately endangered although it nests in a more restricted area than it once did in the Hawaiian Islands.

GALAPAGOS FLIGHTLESS CORMORANT

Nannopterum harrisi

This dark-colored bird of the Galapagos Islands does

Small numbers of this little penguin are still found in the
Galapagos Islands. COURTESY GEORGE LAYCOCK

The flightless cormorant is another of the rare creatures of the Galapagos Islands.   COURTESY GEORGE LAYCOCK

not fly. Each pair will produce one or two eggs each year, and it is believed that there may be only about 1,000 of them left. They have been hunted for meat and eggs in the past and taken for zoo collections.

JAPANESE WHITE STORK   *Ciconia ciconia boyciana*
Once this stork was common in Japan, Korea, Manchuria, and parts of the USSR. Today its range is diminishing. No one knows exactly how many Japanese white storks are still in the area. They are extremely rare. In areas where they remain, the storks have almost no success in reproducing. The problem appears to be due to pesticides. Habitat changes because of drainage have also brought trouble to the Japanese white stork. In addition, people molest them on the nest. The one possibility is that this bird might be saved by captive rearing.

JAPANESE CRESTED IBIS   *Nipponia nippon*
This beautiful bird was common in Japan within the memory of old people there. Today it is seldom seen and must be considered extremely rare. Normally ibis produce two eggs per pair. In 1930, after many years during which this species was believed extinct, a few were rediscovered. The activities of man, in particular the cutting of the forests, caused their troubles.

MEXICAN DUCK   *Anas diazi*
This duck of the southwestern United States and Mexico is gone from some of its former range and rare in other parts. Why? Much of the marshlands where it lived and raised its young has been drained and turned to agricultural crops. Also this duck has hybridized with the common mallard. Fortunately, like many species of waterfowl, the Mexican duck can be raised in captivity.

Consequently it is likely to be saved, if not in the wild, at least in captivity for years to come.

LAYSAN DUCK   *Anas laysanensis*
The little Laysan duck lives only on Laysan Island far out in the Leeward Islands of Hawaii. This is part of the Hawaiian Island National Wildlife Refuge. At one time there may have been only seven of these ducks remaining. Japanese plume hunters almost exterminated them. Later the ducks began to recover. There are perhaps fewer than 200 of them wild on Laysan Island. They are also being reared in captivity.

HAWAIIAN DUCK   *Anas platyrhynchos wyvilliana*
Because of shooting, drainage of fresh water ponds, destruction of marshes, and predatation by imported rats, cats, and mongooses, there may be no more than 500 of these ducks. They are found on only two of the Hawaiian Islands, Kauai and Niihau. If they are to survive in the wild state, some of the wetlands on which they depend must be saved. They are considered to be "rare and decreasing."

ALEUTIAN CANADA GOOSE
                          Branta canadensis leucopareia
Historic home of these small Canada geese is on the foggy Aleutian Islands stretching out from the coast of Alaska toward Russia. Foxes, turned out for fur production, fed heavily on the young and eggs. Now, Buldir Island has been cleared of its fox population, and the geese have been returned to that island in an effort to rebuild the population. Meanwhile other stocks of geese have been released unsuccessfully on Amchitka. They can be raised in captivity, and some are kept at the Patuxent Wildlife Research Center in Maryland.

The Laysan duck, found only on Laysan Island in Hawaii, is in grave danger in the wild.

COURTESY GEORGE LAYCOCK

CALIFORNIA CONDOR   *Gymnogyps californianus*
This giant bird matures at the age of six years, and the female lays only one egg every second year. Some condors have been shot, and others have been poisoned. Some have been so disturbed by intruders that they abandoned their nests. In recent times, efforts have been made to rescue the condor from its approaching extinction. In the Los Padres National Forest there is a condor sanctuary. In addition, these giant birds are protected by law, and there has been widespread publicity to encourage people to help save the last of them.

GALAPAGOS HAWK   *Buteo galapagoensis*
This large, dark-colored hawk was once common throughout many of the Galapagos Islands. Its numbers have diminished because of man's activities there, particularly shooting. Now, it is protected by law and its population, although low, has probably stabilized.

SOUTHERN BALD EAGLE
          Haliaeetus leucocephalus leucocephalus
This spectacular bird, selected as the national emblem of the United States, is believed to be approaching extinction. Once widely distributed over much of northern America, it is now gone from large parts of that original range. Most Americans have never seen a wild bald eagle nor can they hope to. Man has taken over the eagle's range. He has shot the birds, destroyed their nest trees and spread poisons, including DDT, which causes eagles to produce eggs with thin shells. Laws protect the eagles, but they are in serious trouble throughout most of their range.

MONKEY-EATING EAGLE   *Pithecophaga jefferyi*
See text pages.

The Andean condor is a rare giant bird of South America.
COURTESY GEORGE LAYCOCK

RED-BILLED CURASSOW   *Crax blumenbachii*
This is a large, wild fowl of the virgin forests of Brazil. It has long been a favorite with native hunters for food and for feathers to serve as fletching for arrows. Today this bird is probably more rare than the whooping crane and may in fact already be extinct as a wild species.

WESTERN TRAGOPAN   *Tragopan melanocephalus*
Along the border of West Pakistan and India live a small number of these birds. Their numbers are believed to be decreasing, and the sighting of one is a rare occasion. Enemies of the tragopan include destruction of habitat by man and his goats, shooting, and capture of live birds for collectors. These rare birds are now fully protected by law and efforts are being made to reduce them to captivity for release again into a wild habitat where it is hoped the populations can be reestablished.

WHOOPING CRANE   *Grus americana*
This giant bird is one of the most famous of the world's endangered birds. It nests in the Wood Buffalo National Park in northern Canada and winters on the Gulf Coast of Texas in and around the Aransas National Wildlife Refuge. Much publicity has helped reduce the illegal shooting of these remarkable cranes. In recent times their numbers have increased slowly. If protection can continue, a small population of whooping cranes will probably survive for many years.

FLORIDA SANDHILL CRANE   *Grus canadensis pratensis*
This sandhill crane does not migrate but, instead, lives the year around in the wetlands of Florida, southern Georgia's Okefenokee Swamp, and parts of Alabama and Mississippi. Wildlife authorities believe that it is now stable with a population of 2,000 to 3,000. It lays

The whooping crane, one of the best known of the world's rare birds, is shown here at its nest.

COURTESY CHARLES A. KEEFER
U.S. BUREAU OF SPORT FISHERIES AND WILDLIFE

two eggs in a mound made of grass in the marsh. It has been the victim of shooting and egg collecting, as well as the destruction of its habitat for farming. Sanctuaries and refuges now provide it with safe nesting areas, which are important to its future.

PUERTO RICAN PARROT   *Amazona vittata*
    See text pages.

TAKAHE   *Notornis mantelli*
    This large flightless bird was once believed extinct. Today perhaps 300 of them survive in the mountains of New Zealand's South Island. Efforts are being made to protect them in a large refuge there and also to control the predators which men have introduced and which threaten such ground-nesting birds. Even before man moved into the takahe's range, these birds apparently were declining, probably because their habitat was changing faster than they could adapt.

ESKIMO CURLEW   *Numenius borealis*
    Once believed extinct, this very rare shore bird is probably still represented by a small number of individuals. Formerly it bred in northern Canada and Alaska. Those that remain probably spend their winters in the West Indies. During their migrations, flocks of these birds were once shot for the meat markets. There seems little that man can do to help the Eskimo curlew except to continue the legal protection which it has and attempt additional studies to determine its nesting areas.

PUERTO RICAN WHIPPOORWILL
                                Caprimulgus noctitherus
    Men have never known much about this elusive whippoorwill. It was once believed extinct but was rediscov-

ered in 1961. It nests on the ground, where predators, especially the imported mongoose, destroy birds and eggs.

IMPERIAL WOODPECKER *Campephilus imperialis*

This magnificent, big woodpecker lives today only in the very high mountain reaches of the Sierra Madre in Mexico. Its range has shrunk over the years. It has been killed for food and because it was believed to have medicinal powers. By now, it is thought to be nearly extinct. No one knows how many are left. Neither is there much that people are doing, or perhaps can do, for them. Officials believe there are no imperial wood-peckers in captivity and doubt that they would repro-duce in zoos.

IVORY-BILLED WOODPECKER
Campephilus principalis principalis

So rare is this largest of woodpeckers in the United States that it is considered extinct by many ornitholo-gists. Only in a few remote swamp forests is there still hope that remnant numbers may survive. Cutting of the mature forest has destroyed their habitat. If populations are found, refuges might help save the ivory-billed woodpecker.

HAWAIIAN CROW *Corvus tropicus*

Only in one small area on the big island of Hawaii is this crow found. It lives at elevations between 1,000 and 8,000 feet, on the western slope of Mauna Loa. It is seldom seen even by local people. There may be no more than fifty of these crows surviving. Farmers have killed them in past years to protect crops. Today, how-ever, the diminishing Hawaiian crow is protected by law. Ranchers on whose lands they still live are inter-ested in saving them. But their extinction is at hand.

NIHOA MILLERBIRD   *Acrocephalus kingi*
This little brownish, wrenlike bird lives in the bushes and grass on the rocky slopes of Nihoa Island in Hawaii. This island is not inhabited by people and is part of the Hawaiian Islands National Wildlife Refuge, a sanctuary for nesting seabirds. There may be 500 or 600 of these birds on the island. There are none found elsewhere. Fortunately, the island is not infested with such imports as mongooses, rats, cats, or dogs.

MAUI NUKUPUU   *Hemignathus lucidus affinis*
Several species of Hawaii's little forest birds, the honeycreepers, are close to extinction. This one was considered, for many years, to be extinct. But, in 1967, biologists rediscovered a small number of the nukupuu in the mountain wilderness of Maui. As a result, this bird is no longer listed as "extinct," but it is nearly so. What brought it to this may have been imported animals and habitat destruction.

KIRTLAND'S WARBLER   *Dendroica kirtlandii*
This is a large and beautiful warbler with flashy yellow color and a shrill, melodious song. It is known to breed only in one place in the world, the jackpine forests of Michigan's sandhills. In winter, it migrates to the Bahama Islands. A highly specialized bird, it needs young jackpine forests for nesting. Jackpine forests get their start following fire, and now parts of the Huron National Forest are carefully burned regularly for the benefit of the warbler. Even so, its future looks dim, and its numbers are said to be declining.

DUSKY SEASIDE SPARROW   *Ammospiza nigrescens*
This elusive little sparrow lives along the grassy seashore near Cape Kennedy and along the Indian River in

The Kirtland's warbler is an endangered bird that nests only in one small area in Michigan.

COURTESY MICHIGAN DEPARTMENT
OF CONSERVATION

Florida. Hope for the species lies in gaining more information about its life history and needs, and perhaps in establishing additional sanctuaries for it. It has suffered because of habitat destruction.

Reptiles

GIANT TORTOISE　　　　　　　　*Testudo elephantopus*
　　See text pages.

GREEN TURTLE　　　　　　　　*Chelonia mydas mydas*
　　For hundreds of years the green turtle has been a choice food for humans. Not only are the big turtles taken from the sea for meat but their eggs are dug out of the sand. The female green turtle will nest every second or third year and produce 500 or more eggs in a season. The young, however, which hatch 52 to 60 days later, face many kinds of predators. Efforts are being made to establish turtle sanctuaries and move green turtles back to some ancestral nesting areas from which they have been eliminated.

ATLANTIC RIDLEY TURTLE　　　　*Lepidochelys kempii*
　　This rare big turtle of the open sea is under attack from man. Like the alligator, it is taken for its skin. In addition to the valuable turtle leather, the eggs of the Ridley are also stolen. What is needed to save this turtle is better protection from its worst predator—man. Scientists now estimate that there are fewer than 10,000 of these giant sea turtles living. Unless they can be protected, their numbers will almost certainly continue to fall.

AMERICAN ALLIGATOR   *Alligator mississippiensis*

No one knows for certain how many alligators are left. In recent years there has been a growing concern for the future of this giant American reptile. Trouble for the alligator comes from the fact that it wears a skin of value to people. Poachers take them from the swamp to sell their skin on the world market. Recent legislation has brought the species some protection. The alligator is not in danger of immediate extinction, and it is now protected by law in every state where it is found. If poaching can be eliminated, the future of this reptile would seem secure, at least in wildlife refuges and parks.

CHINA ALLIGATOR   *Alligator sinensis*

This cousin of the American alligator is found in small areas of eastern China and especially along the lower Yangtse Valley. It has become extremely rare for the same reasons the American alligator has been disappearing. They are taken for both the meat and skins and also killed because farmers consider them an enemy of livestock.

SPECTACLED CAIMAN   *Caiman crocodilus crocodilus*

This South American reptile is killed in large numbers by hide hunters. The Caimans are reptiles sometimes sold by pet stores as "alligators." This species, native to South America, is found in Venezuela, the Guianas, and the lower Amazon Valley. All species of Caimans, and in fact all the crocodilians in the world, are considered by leading biologists to be endangered.

KOMODO MONITOR   *Varanus komodoensis*

See text pages.

The American alligator is in trouble in many parts of its range.   COURTESY GEORGE LAYCOCK

The Nile crocodile is threatened in Africa.

The land iguana, a large lizard, is one of several endangered animals of the Galapagos Islands in South America.
COURTESY GEORGE LAYCOCK

AMERICAN CROCODILE   *Crocodylus acutus*

This crocodile has a native range from Florida into South America. Throughout that range it is now in danger. A small population of American crocodiles is protected in the Everglades National Park. They have been killed for their skins as well as by people who want to be able to say that they have "killed a croco-dile." They have also been reduced by destruction of their habitat. Like other crocodilians, their future is dim.

NILE CROCODILE   *Crocodylus niloticus*

This famous crocodile of Africa is listed among the world's rare and endangered wild animals. They are taken for their leather by poachers and killed because they are considered a nuisance.

BARRINGTON LAND IGUANA   *Conolophus pallidus*

An estimated 300 of these land iguanas still live on the little island of Santa Cruz in the Galapagos. Natu-ralists visiting this island in recent years have noticed that all of the remaining land iguanas there appear to be old animals. Biologists believe that the imported goats released on the island have been responsible. Goats do not eat these lizards but they do eat the vegetation which once protected the young iguanas by giving them a place to hide from predators. With the vegetation gone, the little iguanas are exposed to the native hawks.

SAN FRANCISCO GARTER SNAKE

Thamnophis sirtalis tetrataenia

Few reptiles are more beautifully marked than this nearly extinct snake. But it is the victim of advancing civilization. Man's housing developments, drainage proj-ects, and land clearing have destroyed its natural habitat and left it few places to live. There are no more than a few of these snakes in captivity and little is being done in their behalf. What is needed is to have acreages of wetland habitat set aside in their native California range.

AMPHIBIANS

TEXAS BLIND SALAMANDER　　*Typhlomolge rathbuni*

Among the rarest animals in North America is this little cave-dwelling salamander. It is known to inhabit only a few places in Hays County, Texas. According to the U.S. Bureau of Sport Fisheries and Wildlife, it is nearly extinct. There are two major reasons. First, the limited habitat has been destroyed by lowering of underground water tables. Meanwhile, salamanders are so rare, collectors have pursued the last of them. There is very little chance of saving this tiny animal in captivity because it does not do well when taken from its native caves. The only ray of hope comes from the Texas Chapter of the Nature Conservancy, which has purchased Ezell's Cave to save it for the salamander.

VEGAS VALLEY LEOPARD FROG　　*Rana pipiens fisheri*

This frog which evolved around springs in the vicinity of Las Vegas, Nevada, may already be extinct. Much of its former habitat has been destroyed by man's water control structures. In addition, both trout and bullfrogs introduced into the area feed on the young of the frog. Not since 1942, according to the U.S. Department of the Interior, has one of these frogs been seen in its natural habitat by a biologist.

FISH

ATLANTIC SALMON　　*Salmo salar*

See text pages.

Organizations Concerned with Endangered Wildlife

American Association of Zoological Parks and Aquariums, 1700 Pennsylvania Avenue, N.W., Washington, D.C. 20006

American Ornithologists' Union, Smithsonian Institution, Washington, D.C. 20560

American Society of Mammologists, Bryan P. Glass, Secretary-Treasurer, Dept. of Zoology, Oklahoma State University, Stillwater, Oklahoma 74074

Boone & Crockett Club, c/o Carnegie Museum, Pittsburgh, Pennsylvania

Defenders of Wildlife, 2000 N Street, N.W., Washington, D.C. 20036

Fauna Preservation Society, Zoological Society of London, N.W.L., 4 RY, England

International Union for Conservation of Nature and Natural Resources, 1110 Morges, Switzerland

Izaak Walton League of America, 1800 N. Kent Street, Suite 806, Arlington, Virginia 22209

National Audubon Society, 950 Third Avenue, New York, New York 10022

National Parks and Conservation Association, 1701 18th St., N.W., Washington, D.C. 20009

National Wildlife Federation, 1412 16th Street, N.W., Washington, D.C. 20036

Nature Conservancy, The, 800 N. Kent Street, Arlington, Virginia 22209

Sierra Club, 1050 Mills Towers, San Francisco, California 94104

Sport Fishing Institute, Suite 503, 719 13th Street, N.W. Washington, D.C. 20005

Whooping Crane Conservation Association, Inc., R.R. 1, Box 485A, Kula, Maui, Hawaii 96790

Wildlife Society, The, Suite S-176, 3900 Wisconsin Avenue, N.W., Washington, D.C. 20016

Wildlife Management Institute, 709 Wire Building, Washington, D.C. 20005

Wilderness Society, The, 729 15th Street, N.W., Washington, D.C. 20005

World Wildlife Fund, 910 17th Street, N.W., Washington, D.C. 20036

BIBLIOGRAPHY

Allen, Glover M., *Extinct and Vanishing Mammals of the Western Hemisphere*. American Committee for International Wildlife Protection, Spec. Publ. II, 1942.

Allen, Robert P., *The Whooping Crane*. National Audubon Society Research Report No. 3, 1963. (Republished by Dover Publications, New York, 1966.)

Brown, Leslie, and Amadon, Dean, *Eagles, Hawks and Falcons of the World*. Vols. I and II, Country Life Books, Feltham, England, 1968.

Cahalane, V.H., "Status of the Black-Footed Ferret." *Journal of Mammalogy*, 35: 418-242 (1954).

Crowe, Philip Kingsland, *The Empty Ark*. New York: Charles Scribner's Sons, 1967.

Dufresne, Frank, "Plight of the Ice Bear." *Audubon Magazine*, 68: 418-242 (1966).

Fisher, James; Simon, Noel; and Vincent, Jack, *Wildlife in Danger*. New York: The Viking Press, Inc., 1969.

Greenway, J.C., Jr., *Extinct and Vanishing Birds of the World.* New York: American Committee for International Wildlife Protection, 1958.

Grimwood, Ian, "Operation Oryx." *Oryx,* 6 (6): 308-334 (1962).

——————— "Operation Oryx: The Second Stage." Oryx, 7 (5): 223-225 (1964).

——————— "Operation Oryx: The Three Stages of Captive Breeding." *Oryx,* 9 (2): 110-118 (1967).

Harrington, C.R., "The Life and Status of the Polar Bear." *Oryx,* 8 (3): 169-176 (1965).

Jackson, Peter (ed.), *World Wildlife Yearbook 1970-71.* Morges, Switzerland: World Wildlife Fund, 1971.

Koford, Carl B., *The California Condor.* National Audubon Society Research Report No. 3, 1953 (Republished by Dover Publications, 1966.)

Laycock, George, *America's Endangered Wildlife.* New York: Grosset & Dunlap, Inc., 1969.

——————— *Animal Movers.* New York: Doubleday & Co., Inc., 1971.

McMillan, Ian, *Man and the California Condor.* New York: E.P. Dutton & Co., Inc., 1968.

McNulty, Faith, *The Whooping Crane.* New York: E.P. Dutton & Co., Inc., 1966.

Milton, Oliver, "The Orangutan and Rhinoceros in North Sumatra." *Oryx,* 7 (4): 177-184 (1964).

Perry, Richard, *The World of the Polar Bear.* London: Cassell & Co., Ltd., 1966.

Pimlott, D.H., "The Status and Distribution of the Red Wolf." (Trans.) North American Wildlife Conf. 33: 373-389 (1968).

Roosevelt, Kermit, "The Search for the Giant Panda." *Natural History* 30 (1): 3-16 (1930).

Sage, Dean, "In Quest of the Giant Panda." *Natural History* 35 (4): 309-320 (1935).

Schaller, George B., *The Mountain Gorilla, Ecology and Behavior.* Chicago: University of Chicago Press, 1963.

——————— "The Tiger and Its Prey." *Natural History* 75 (8): 30-37 (1966).

Schuhmacher, E. *The Last Paradises.* Garden City, New York: Doubleday & Co., Inc., 1967.

Scott, Peter, (ed.), *The Launching of a New Ark, First Report of the World Wildlife Fund.* Morges, Switzerland: World Wildlife Fund, 1965.

Simon, Noel, and Geroudt, Paul, *Last Survivors.* New York: The World Publishing Co., 1970.

Simon, Noel, "Of Whales and Whaling." *Science* 149 (3687): 943-946 (1965).

——————— Red Data Book, Vol. 1, *Mammalia,* 1966. International Union for Conservation of Nature and Natural Resources. Also other volumes on Birds, Fish, Amphibians and Reptiles.

Stott, Ken, Jr., and Selsor, C. J., "The Orangutan in North Borneo." *Oryx* 6 (1): 39-42 (1961).

Tanner, James T., *The Ivory-Billed Woodpecker.* National Audubon Society Research Report No. 1, 1942. (Republished by Dover Publications, New York, 1966.)

Vollman, Fritz, (ed.), *The Ark Underway, Second Report of the World Wildlife Fund 1965-1967.* (1966.). Morges, Switzerland: World Wildlife Fund, 1968. *World Wildlife Yearbook 1968.* Morges, Switzerland: World Wildlife Fund, 1969. *World Wildlife Fund Yearbook 1969.* Morges, Switzerland: World Wildlife Fund, 1969.

INDEX

148